Etiquette

COLLINS NUTSHELL BOOKS

Etiquette

MARTINE LEGGE

COLLINS
LONDON AND GLASGOW

First published 1964
This facsimile edition published 2009
ISBN 978-0-00-729557-9

Contents

"Oh what agony the mind assails
when one's the only one in tails
and can the horror be forgot
when one's the only one who's not?

"One lives one's life in constant terror
of perpetrating just one error
but the fear which makes my senses dumb
to be the *only* one to come."

ANON.

FOREWORD

Etiquette is a means, not an end. It is a code of behaviour governing everyday activities which brings some order into relationships with other people. Etiquette (which really means good manners) will never turn you into a saint or a genius, but it will facilitate your passage through life and may enable you to achieve a position which a genius might easily fail to gain because he is a boor and antagonises others. Pleasant, helpful, amiable people who never jar or hurt others, who are considerate and peacemaking, are of great value in any society.

Manners are not always noticeable when they are good. It is when they are bad that they not only arouse anger or displeasure, but draw the attention of onlookers to all the *other* faults their perpetrator may possess!

Manners should always be smooth and easy. They should become part of one's personality and should not be mugged up before a party like facts before an examination, or they will appear contrived and false. A medieval Italian once said that civility becomes ponderous once it ceases to be gay.

You might think that some points of etiquette are utterly unreasonable or without any basis. Raising hats (a left-over from the days when knights *had* to raise their visors in order to be able to talk at all) and the use of certain expressions considered to be correct while others are, for no good reason, considered common, are two examples. Society is rather like a club. For better or for worse, if you wish to belong you must conform to the rules. You may well ask why you should conform. We live in a conformist world, however, and throughout history every group of people calling itself a society has conformed to *something*, from the taboos of primitive tribes to the status symbols of today. Good manners constitute a far greater status symbol than large cars and mink coats. Furthermore, they cost absolutely nothing!

Codes of manners have always preoccupied civilisations, societies and even great men. Confucius considered it rude to point. Cicero thought the only occupation for a "real gentleman" was the pursuit of agriculture. Erasmus had some excellent ideas about manners which included the firm belief that one must not gossip, tell unkind stories, shout or mumble. One must never be too inquisitive or indulge in self-display. One must be discreet and admit to nothing which might be an embarrassment if repeated. He was a great philosopher who was mainly concerned with deeper thoughts, but his dictums might well have been those of a Lady Hortensia Bloggs or any of those thousand other serious ladies who laid down the law during the 19th century, that age of banal refinements in the "do's and don'ts" of good behaviour.

Rules of etiquette change, of course, from generation to generation. Life changes and it would be foolish to retain customs which are redundant and do not fit in with other new ideas, but the basis of kindness and consideration for others never changes. While visiting cards are rapidly disappearing, writing thank-you letters has never ceased to be encouraged. You can see the difference between these two points of etiquette. One is ageless and the other is a custom of the moment. Good manners, basically, mean that you will *appear* to be equally charming whether you are feeling angelically good-tempered or diabolically out-of-sorts.

Emphasis on various points also changes from generation to generation. In a book of Elizabethan etiquette you would have been told not to wipe your mouth on your sleeve or pick your teeth with a penknife, and if your sleeves fall into the soup, to pin them up immediately. Nowadays this kind of advice is unnecessary, because for generations we have learnt to eat better, but we could all do with reminders of how to behave on the telephone.

Manners also tend to wax and wane with periods of affluence and wars. In 1692 they were so bad that a society was founded for the reformation of good manners. We are in the midst of a period today when we are picking ourselves up from the laxity of post-war behaviour; yet we are right to discard many contrived and redundant customs which do not fit in with modern life. In this book, I have tried to do two things: to give *practical* help for all social occasions, and to explain why certain customs are being discarded whilst others are still as important as ever.

1

WRITING LETTERS

Writing a letter is communicating with another person without the help of physical charm or the stimulus and exchange of conversation; therefore it is something which needs extra care and thought if you are to give the right impression of yourself, your education and your background. Yet, in an age of increasingly better education, few put themselves across to their best advantage on paper. This is mostly due to a careless approach. It is not so much a matter of writing with grandiloquence as of writing clearly and concisely without losing the charm of your own particular brand of personality. Gone are the stilted letters of yesterday. You can write as freely as you like, but write, do not telegraph your feelings or message. A good letter is written as you might speak, but with a little more polish and division of ideas into paragraphs.

A good letter is also dependent to a certain extent upon presentation or layout, as in a newspaper or magazine. The matter should be easy to read and attractively set out, with fair margins and space between the paragraphs. In business a letter sells, impresses and informs. (A letter of application for instance, is your personal advertisement.) In private matters a letter can give the greatest pleasure, maintaining friendships and keeping alive a web of relationships almost better than the telephone. A letter, however short, is always more courteous and more of a personal compliment than a telephone call. It gives the impression that you have taken more trouble.

Materials

Black or dark blue ink on white paper looks best: the greater the contrast, the cleaner the layout, the easier it is to read. You can get away with grey or azure paper but avoid other colours. For no logical reason, they are considered "not the done thing." Single sheets are used today more often than the folded kind. Avoid crinkly edges, lined paper and "dinky" sizes. Never use coloured inks unless you are drawing a diagram or have an established reputation as an eccentric! Thank-you letters, letters of condolence, and business letters of a personal nature should not be typed.

Layout

The letterhead or address should be in the centre or the top right-hand corner of the page, at best engraved in a dark colour. If you cannot afford this, have it printed in black on white paper. This, if well done, resembles engraving. The date should be written below this on the right-hand side, except when answering an invitation in the third person; then it goes on the bottom left-hand corner. Always leave a margin of about an inch all round the sheet of paper.

In business letters or any communication with a shop or firm, the name of the person to whom you are writing or his title, according to the position he holds in the firm, should be written or typed on the left-hand side of the letter just above the salutation, together with the name and address of the firm. Thus:

> The Managing Director
> Smith Paper Works,
> Gnome Road,
> Preston, Lancs.

If you address anyone by name, put his title under his name, e.g. A. J. Bloggs, Esq.,
                    Managing Director.
This is principally to make filing easier.

Addressing Envelopes

It is customary today to address a man as John Smith Esq., rather than Mr. Smith. This is because the title has lost its true significance along the years. It is a courtesy title dating from medieval times and meant to denote a man of gentle birth, although Esquire was officially a rank above that of a mere gentleman. Today, when class differences, apart from the aristocracy, are mostly a matter of money, and families move in and out of various classes with each generation, there is no reason to deny a man a courtesy which is devoid of any real meaning. Americans and those who live in the Dominions usually prefer to be addressed as Mr. on the envelope, unless they are the kind of snobs who regard anything British as the acme of good breeding! It is correct to write to a tradesman as Mr. in a business communication, but if you write to him in any other capacity (for instance, if he is a local councillor) you then address him as Esq., as you would on a personal letter.

Anyone possessing civil or military decorations, crown honours, or letters denoting professional or official status should have these added after the Esq. Thus J.P. for Justice of the Peace; O.B.E. for Order of the British Empire; M.P. for Member of Parliament; Q.C. for Queen's Counsel, and membership of learned societies such as F.R.S. for Fellow of the Royal Society; R.A. for Royal Academician; F.R.G.S. for Fellow of the Royal Geographical Society; F.B.A. for Fellow of the British Academy, and others. University degrees of Master of

Arts, Bachelor of Arts or Bachelor of Science (M.A., B.A. and B.Sc.) are not added after the name on personal letters, only on professional letters. A surgeon should be addressed on the envelope as John Smith Esq., F.R.C.S., and a doctor as John Smith Esq., M.D. or whatever his degree may be, although it is also correct to address the latter as Dr. John Smith on the envelope.

Do not gild the lily by adding strings of letters after a man's name, just put the most important. If you are writing to someone and you suspect he may have such a status or decoration, you can look him up in the many reference books dealing with the professions, aristocracy, or people of note (such as *Who's Who*). These can be found in any public library.

A Married Woman should be addressed on the envelope by using her husband's first name or initials before the surname, thus Mrs. James Grant or Mrs. J. S. Grant. This is purely social etiquette as in law she retains her first name and initials, using them on her passport, share certificates and in business. A divorced woman is addressed by her first name before the surname, while a widow still has the right to use her husband's first name. If she has a title and a son who inherits his father's title, however, she may then be addressed as Ethel, Lady Smith or Ethel, Countess of Blank.

Clergymen of all denominations are referred to on the envelope as "The Rev.", e.g. The Rev. John Jones, unless they are Rabbis of the Jewish faith, and then they are addressed as "The Rev. Rabbi Cohen." (For canons, bishops, etc., *see pages 32-4*.)

For Boys "Master" has fallen into disuse. Today it is

correct to write to a boy at school as James Smith, and after the age of 16 or thereabouts as James Smith, Esq.

Beginnings and Endings

Most letters begin "Dear Mr. Smith," "Dear Sir," "Dear Mary." "My dear" is more friendly (although this is the other way around in the United States), and usually used in a letter from an older person to a younger or between people of the same age, but not in a letter from a younger to an older person. Formal letters, or letters written to someone with whom you are not well acquainted, should end "Yours sincerely." "Yours very sincerely" does not mean anything and should be avoided as being mannered, although "Best wishes" or "Kindest regards" written on the line above "Yours sincerely" softens the ending and sounds more friendly when you know the person to whom you are writing.

When you know someone really very well but do not wish to end "With love from," you can write "Yours" or "Yours ever." Such letters should be signed with your first name only. "Yours affectionately" instead of "Love from" is an attractive way of ending a letter, especially from an older person to a younger.

Business Letters or letters to the bank manager, inspector of taxes, letters answering advertisements or complaining to the manager of a store should start "Dear Sir" and end "Yours faithfully." "Dear Sirs" is used when writing to a corporate body such as a shop. Business letters addressed to someone you know, or to whom you have been given an introduction, should begin "Dear Mr. Smith" and end "Yours sincerely." Business letters to women you do not know are addressed "Dear Madam."

An American habit which is sometimes used in this

country when writing to professional people such as writers, artists or editors, is to address them as "Dear Mary Jones" or "Dear John Smith." I have never known anyone who is not infuriated by this and it is wise to avoid this form of address.

To begin a letter "Sir" is very formal and only rarely used in letters written in an official capacity to mayors, heads of organisations, members of the peerage or the editor of a newspaper, when you wish to emphasise the seriousness of the letter's contents and hope to get it published. Such letters should end "I am, Sir, Yours faithfully." But professional letters, as opposed to business letters, should end, "I am, Sir, Yours truly." Letters addressed to an official body and beginning "Gentlemen" should end "I am, Gentlemen, Yours truly."

Never sign a letter "Mrs. Jones" or "Mr. Jones" but give your full first name and surname, or initials in the case of a business letter, if you prefer it. When a woman writes to a shop or an organisation where it would not be known whether she is married or single, it is correct to print on the bottom left-hand corner, level with her signature, "Mrs. J. S. Jones" or "Miss J. S. Jones." Never put "Mrs." in brackets beside your name.

Special Letters

Thank-you Letters. Far too few of them are written today. Not only are they a courtesy but a great source of pleasure to the recipient. For the cost of a postage stamp and a few minutes of your time this is one of the ways to gain a reputation as a person who is well-mannered and thoughtful.

All formal dinner parties should be followed by a letter of thanks, however brief, not a postcard or one of those "notelets." You should also thank for a formal luncheon. If you have particularly enjoyed an informal dinner party with friends, it is kind and courteous to write a note saying so. Nor is this a suggestion for women only, although married women always write on behalf of themselves and their husbands. A single man invited to a dinner party should also write a brief letter or send flowers with his thanks on a card. (Never underestimate the effect of such a gesture on the wife of a business acquaintance who has given you a meal on terms of business rather than friendship!) Always write to the hostess and address the envelope to her. You can, of course, thank her and her husband in the body of your letter. If the hosts are great personal friends a telephone call will do, although a letter is always a greater courtesy. Nor is it strange today to refer to the excellence of the meal as it was years ago. For hostesses have to do most of the hard work themselves, and it is a delight to be told their efforts have been appreciated.

You should always write a thank-you letter for a week-end spent in someone else's home or for a gift of any kind. These letters should be written the following day. It is courteous to thank anyone who has given you an interview or written or telephoned a reference or an introduction, especially if it was at your request. They will also be pleased if you tell them the results of any trouble they may have taken on your behalf.

It is not necessary to write thank-you letters for cocktail parties, large receptions such as buffet parties or wedding receptions unless you particularly wish to do so. Take nothing for granted, and you will never be lacking in good manners. No thank-you letter is ever out of place.

Letters of Introduction and References. Should you give a letter to a friend introducing him to a business acquaintance or another friend abroad, to use when he needs (he may not get there for some time), you do not seal it; just push in the flap and write "By hand" on the envelope. The person whom it introduces should send it with a covering note to the person to whom it is addressed. He should not push it into his hand at their first meeting. This is merely embarrassing.

Another method of introduction is to write to your friend saying that so-and-so will call on him, explaining why and asking for his help and co-operation. It is, however, imperative to warn a friend or acquaintance that someone is going to call upon him, and to give a reason for the introduction and tell him what kind of person he may expect. In the old days it was an unwritten law that both sides should be agreeable to the introduction before it was effected. Today this custom has fallen into abeyance. The least you can do is to give a warning, as well as to be sure that you are not causing offence or being a nuisance.

When you secure a job or whatever it is the reference or letter of introduction has helped you to do, it is courteous to write and tell your referee and to thank him.

Should you want to give someone's name for a reference you must always ask his permission first. Anyone who has not been asked has the right to be angry, as it implies that you are taking him for granted.

Letters of Complaint. These should be short and courteous. Never let your anger get out of hand. Make the letter very formal and list your complaints. Ask for an explanation. Never threaten or allow yourself to be rude. Apart from common courtesy, this is dangerous and may land you in a court of law. A letter is proof for ever of the words you are saying, and cannot be forgotten or denied as can a conversation or telephone call. Be absolutely sure that you are in the right and give the other party the benefit of the doubt, intimating that you are sure he will do everything in his power to put things right. If you cannot get satisfaction and the situation is grave enough, ask your solicitor for advice.

Letters of Condolence. These letters are difficult to write. The only point of such a letter is to extend your deepest sympathy and to offer any kind of help, companionship or affection which the situation allows, and in accordance with the closeness of your relationship. Write briefly and make the bereaved person feel that he is not forsaken in a world which neither shares nor understands his sorrow. This type of letter requires a certain amount of trouble and thought. You need not write a long catalogue listing the qualities of the deceased, although by all means say something nice and how much you will miss him.

Letters about Jobs. If you are answering an advertisement, address the letter to the personnel officer or whoever is indicated in the advertisement. Begin "Dear Sir" or "Dear Madam." Say why you are interested in that particular job, briefly what you are doing at the moment and why you wish to change. Take care not to run down your present job or company: this looks bad. Say that you would like an interview, and if there is any time of day when you could not possibly get away, explain why. Write the letter in your own handwriting and, without familiarity, try to include a little of your sparkle and personality. You should attach a typed *curriculum vitae*. This states your date of birth, the schools you have attended, and any diplomas or degrees you may have gained. Then list the various jobs you have held, giving dates. Write a paragraph about any particular achievements or

19

experiences, e.g. published works, community or social work, flying licence, languages and their fluency. Say something about hobbies or any of your special interests. All this gives some idea of the kind of person you are and how you get on with the world around you.

There is no reason why you should state your religion and it is impertinence for an employer to ask; but say whether you are single or married and if you have any children.

At this point you need not give the names and addresses of those willing to give you a reference. When references are requested, ask permission of those whose names you wish to give, and then write giving the names and addresses of those who have agreed.

A good letter of application is one of the best entries to a job, even if you write out of the blue, hoping there may be a job vacant although you have seen no advertisement. Even if a job is not available at the moment of writing, your letter may impress a firm enough for the managing director or personnel officer to ask you to come along for an interview. Just think of all the *other* letters piling up on the desks of future employers, and make sure that yours at least is a paragon in so far as materials, layout and writing are concerned. Do not become long-winded, but do not be so brief that you sound off-hand and give no inkling of your personality.

Always write a letter accepting a post the day you receive the offer of the job you have applied for. You should mention the terms, pay, hours, holidays and say you accept them. End with a sincere wish that you will do your best and are sure that you will enjoy the job.

2

CARDS

Postcards

Those of a pictorial nature are strictly for holidays. A correspondence card with your name, address and telephone number printed across the top and underlined can be used for brief communications (confirming time of arrival, informal invitations and acceptances and all kinds of messages which are not of a personal nature). You never write "dear so-and-so" on a postcard, but start right off with your message.

A married man usually uses his wife's cards for private correspondence. He merely crosses out the "Mrs." It is unusual for a single man to have them printed under his name. Such a card looks like this:

From: Mrs. John Smith, 41 Arno Close, Pacton, Hants.
Tel: Pacton 561

Christmas Cards have many pros and cons in a modern world. Basically, they are a greeting at a feast which, among other things, is a symbol of goodwill and renewed friendship. Therefore it is lacking in courtesy and out of spirit to send a card with your name printed inside and no written signature (and this applies to business cards as well). Christmas cards provide an excellent opportunity to renew old friendships which have fallen by the wayside, or to maintain ties of affection with friends you may not see very often. In this case a personal message, however brief, is courteous and kind. It is quite unnecessary to send cards to people you see every day, as in the office.

Apart from birthday cards, all other kinds of congratulation should be made in a letter and not conveyed via the printed "joke" cards which are on sale at most stationers. Should you want to send one of these, let it be a joke and only for your close family and friends.

Visiting Cards

The custom of leaving visiting cards has fallen into disuse and rightly so, because it was truly one of the most complicated and contrived pieces of etiquette. Today, if people wish to call, they telephone first to see if a time is convenient, or they send a letter to a newcomer in the district inviting him or her to come round for a drink or coffee.

It is still perfectly correct, however, to have your own cards, because they are useful for exchanging addresses at parties or to accompany any gift such as a wedding present or a bunch of flowers (a personal message should always be written on the back), or to be attached to a wreath at a funeral. Men and women use cards in exactly the same way, although a business card which carries the name of the man's firm should never be used on social occasions. Cards are left at the British Embassy when you are abroad on business.

Cards should be engraved in black copperplate or small block letters with your name "Mrs., Miss or Lady Bloggs" in the centre and the address in smaller letters at the bottom left-hand corner. For a man, "Mr. John Bloggs," "Captain J. D. Bloggs, R.N." or "Sir John Bloggs," without adding orders, decorations or degrees is correct. A doctor's card reads "Dr. J. D. Bloggs," and an army officer puts the name of his regiment in smaller type below his name. Cards should be white and not too thick. A woman's is slightly larger than a man's.

Invitations for week-ends, ordinary dinner parties and to a few friends for drinks are issued by letter or on the telephone as the occasion may warrant. They should be sent two weeks to eight days prior to the date of the party. For week-ends longer notice should be given.

Invitations to weddings, dances, large cocktail parties and sometimes formal dinners are issued by card. Invitations to weddings and formal dinners go out in the names of both host and hostess. Other invitations are in the name of the hostess. The envelope is addressed to one person only—to the wife in the case of a married couple, although the invitation inside is addressed to both of them.

A Wedding Invitation is printed or, if you are feeling rich, engraved in black on a folded sheet of thick white paper, absolutely plain with no silver or fluted edges. Replies are written by hand in the third person. A wedding invitation is sent out by the bride's parents about six weeks before the wedding and should read as follows:

Major and Mrs. John Smith
request the pleasure of
your company at the marriage
of their daughter
MARY JANE
to
MR. ROY JONES
at St. Mary's Church, Maplehurst
on Wednesday, May 2nd at 2.30 o'clock
and afterwards at
the Bell Hotel.

R.S.V.P.
Oldfield Hall,
Maplehurst,
Kent.

The names of the guests are written by the hostess on the top left-hand corner of the invitation.

The reply should be written in a block in the centre of a sheet of writing paper as follows:

> Mr. and Mrs. Ronald Jones have much pleasure in accepting the kind invitation of Major and Mrs. John Smith to the marriage of their daughter at St. Mary's Church, Maplehurst, on Wednesday, May 2nd, and afterwards at the Bell Hotel.

A refusal can read as follows:

> Mr. and Mrs. Ronald Jones regret that they are unable to accept the kind invitation of Major and Mrs. John Smith to the marriage of their daughter at St. Mary's Church, Maplehurst, on Wednesday, May 2nd, as they will be away.

It is, however, not necessary to give any excuse at all. The date is written on the bottom left-hand corner of the sheet of writing paper, and the envelope is addressed to the hostess alone.

Invitation by Card to Cocktail and Other Parties. This is always an "At Home" card. If you can afford it, and give many parties of this kind, you can have cards printed with your name at the top and address on the bottom left-hand corner, with spaces left for names of guests the kind of party, time and date. Like this:

Mrs. James Smith

AT HOME

....

R.S.V.P.
Hay Lodge,
Midhurst,
Sussex.

The day of the week and the date is written under the AT HOME, and the kind of party and the time is written on the bottom right-hand corner. "Cocktails, 6.30—8.30 p.m." or "Wine and cheese, 8.30 p.m." or "Dancing and buffet supper, 9.30—1 a.m."

Most people buy plain "At Home" cards from a stationer, and on these spaces are left for the hostess to fill in everything herself.

Answers to such invitations should be written in the third person, repeating the date, place and time of the party:

Mr. and Mrs. John Smith accept with pleasure Mrs. James Finche's invitation to cocktails on Saturday, 4th December, at 6.30 p.m.

For formal Dinner Parties and if you are feeling rather grand, you may send an "At Home" card filled in as for other parties but with the words "Dinner, 7.45 p.m." on the bottom right-hand corner. Presumably you will also want your guests to dress, so you will add beneath the time "Black tie," which means that the men will wear dinner jackets and the women cocktail dresses or short evening dresses. You can also write in the third person on a piece of writing paper:

Mr. and Mrs. James Smith
request the pleasure of
the company of
MR. JOHN FINCH
at dinner on
Saturday, 12th February
at eight o'clock.

R.S.V.P.
8 Formby Gardens,
S.W.5.

But most dinner party invitations are issued by letter or on the telephone.

A Special Dance, such as a coming out dance or a 21st birthday dance, will probably entice you to spend the money to have special invitations printed as for a wedding. They are printed on cards as follows:

Mrs. John Smith
AT HOME
Friday, January 8th
at the Hyde Park Hotel.

R.S.V.P.
31 Holly Close,
Hampstead,
N.W.3.

Dancing 10 p.m.
Black tie.

To write the time as "o'clock" used to be thought much grander than writing p.m. or a.m., but this is now nonsense and hostesses may put what they wish.

Sometimes the word "Decorations" appears at the bottom of an invitation, usually to a formal reception at an embassy or when members of the Royal Family will be present, or at official receptions given by Cabinet Ministers, Lord Mayors or Lord-Lieutenants of the County. This means the men will wear evening dress with whatever orders and decorations they are entitled to. If they have miniature medals they wear these. Women wear full evening dress and long gloves.

All invitations should be replied to within 48 hours so that a hostess can make other arrangements if you cannot accept. This rule is not so stringent for wedding invitations, but these should be answered within a week.

General Points

The names of guests are always written by hand on the top left-hand corner of the invitation. Thus, "Miss Mary Smith" or "Mr. and Mrs. John Smith." Any children invited (to a wedding for instance), have their names written underneath their parents' as "Miss Mary Smith" and, underneath again, "Miss Caroline Smith." If two sisters are being asked, the name of the younger is written beneath that of her elder sister. A brother's name is written beneath the name of his sister. The names of Peers, Baronets and Knights are written: "Lord and Lady Bloggs," or "Sir James and Lady Bloggs." Only a Duke and Duchess are written out as "The Duke and Duchess of Bloggs." The prefix "Hon." is never used except on the envelope—plain Mr., Mrs. or Miss is written before the names.

3

FORMS OF ADDRESS

Royalty and Nobility

When introduced to royalty, women curtsy and men bow. They also do this if a royal personage walks past them at a garden party or at a film première. In the first spoken reply you should always say "Your Majesty" or "Your Royal Highness." After the first reply (it is protocol that royalty always addresses the other person first), you need only say "Sir" or "Madam." This applies to Kings, Queens, Royal Princesses and Princes and Royal Dukes and Duchesses.

On the whole, letters should not be addressed personally to members of the Royal Family unless you know them. They should be addressed to the lady-in-waiting or private secretary, asking them to submit your request or thanks or whatever it is you wish to say to the royal personage. These letters should open "Sir" or "Madam," and end "I have the honour to be, Sir (or Madam), your obedient servant." The envelope is addressed to:

The Private Secretary to *or* The Lady-In-Waiting to

H.R.H. Princess Alexandra.

An invitation to a royal garden-party is issued by the Lord Chamberlain as a royal command from the Queen. These invitations do not require replies unless serious illness or a very serious excuse prevent your attending.

28

Then your explanation is sent to the official who issues the invitation, in this case the Lord Chamberlain.

For any other invitation to appear before royalty you reply to the official who issues the invitation card.

"Mrs. James Finch presents her compliments to the Lord Chamberlain and will be honoured to obey Her Majesty's gracious command to . . ."

There are seven degrees of rank in this country which carry a title. They are: Duke, Marquis, Earl, Viscount, Baron, Baronet, Knight. The first five are peers of the realm and sit in the House of Lords. Baronet may sometimes be a very ancient title, but Baronets are not noblemen and do not have any rights other than handing their titles on to their sons. Knights hold their titles only for their lifetime.

There is a slight difference in the way titled persons are addressed in *business* letters as opposed to purely *social* letters. On the envelopes of business letters, they are all (including their wives) "The Right Hon." addressed as:

> The Right Hon. The Marquess of . . . or
> > The Marchioness of . . .
> The Right Hon. The Earl of . . . or
> > The Countess of . . .
> The Right Hon. The Viscount . . . or
> > The Viscountess . . .
> The Right Hon. The Lord . . .
> > The Lady . . . (Baroness)

On the envelopes of *social* letters "The Right Hon." is dropped. Dukes and Duchesses are addressed on the envelopes of business letters as: "His Grace the Duke of " . . . or "Her Grace the Duchess of. . . ."

In business letters, the salutation (including that to a Duke and Duchess) is "Sir" or "Madam," ending "I am, Sir, (or Madam), Yours faithfully. . . ."

A Duke and Duchess are addressed in social letters, provided you move in the same social circles, as "Dear Duke" or "My Dear Duchess" or "Dear Duchess", if you are a friend rather than acquaintance. You end the letter "Yours sincerely." On official occasions they are addressed in introductions and on platforms as "His Grace," "Her Grace" or "Your Grace." On purely social occasions when a Duke and Duchess are being entertained, you would introduce a commoner to the Duchess as "Miss Jones: the Duchess of Bloggs," and in conversation address her as "Duchess," although in English we have that delicious word "You." With care, a person's title need never be mentioned except when introducing them!

The daughters of Dukes are "Lady," e.g. "Lady Mary Jones." They keep their titles even if they marry commoners, becoming, for instance, "Lady Mary Smith." They are introduced as "Lady Mary Smith," and spoken to as "Lady Mary."

The sons of Dukes have the courtesy title of "Lord," which is used with their Christian names and family names; thus "Lord John Manners." Their wives become "Lady John Manners" and are addressed in speech as "Lady John." The eldest son of a Duke takes his father's second title and is addressed as if he were a peer, although he does not sit in the House of Lords.

A Marquess and Marchioness are addressed in social letters as "Dear Lord Bloggs" or "Dear Lady Bloggs." In conversation they are referred to and addressed as "Lord and Lady Bloggs."

The eldest son of a Marquess takes his father's second title which is usually that of an Earl. Younger sons have the courtesy title of "Honourable". Daughters of Marquesses are "Lady Caroline Smith," and keep their titles even if they marry commoners. They are addressed in the same way as the daughters of Dukes.

An Earl and Countess are addressed in social letters as "Dear Lord Bloggs" or "Lady Bloggs," and in conversation as "Lord and Lady Bloggs." The eldest son of an Earl takes his father's second title, which is either that of Viscount or Baron, and younger sons have the courtesy title of "The Hon. John Bloggs," although this is never used except on an envelope. The daughters of Earls have the title of "Lady" and remain "Lady Mary" even if they marry commoners, merely taking on their husband's surname. They are addressed as "Lady Mary" in conversation, and introduced as "Lady Mary Bloggs." In social letters, they are addressed as "Dear Lady Mary," as are the daughters of Dukes and Marquesses.

Viscounts, Viscountesses, Barons and Baronesses are addressed in social letters as "Dear Lord Bloggs" or "Dear Lady Bloggs," and similarly in conversation. All their sons and daughters are styled "The Hon. John (or Mary) Bloggs" on the envelopes of letters, retaining this prefix even if they marry commoners. Thus the daughter of a Baron who marries a Mr. Smith is "The Hon. Mrs. Smith." "The Hon." is used only on an envelope or in a newspaper or formal announcement. Unmarried daughters and sons are not addressed on envelopes as Mr. and Miss but as "The Hon. Caroline Bloggs" or "The Hon. John Bloggs." When daughters marry, they become "The Hon. Mrs. Smith" or, if they marry a Baronet or Knight, "The Hon. Lady Smith." Sons continue to be addressed on the envelope as "The Hon. John Bloggs," and their wives are addressed on the envelope as "The Hon. Mrs. John Bloggs."

Children of "Life" peers do not have any titles.

A Baronet (whose title is hereditary) is addressed on the envelope as "Sir John Smith, Bart. (or Bt.)." His wife is "Lady Smith." He is addressed in conversation as "Sir John," although his wife is addressed as "Lady Smith" both in conversation and in a letter. The children have no courtesy titles.

A Knight's title (there are seven different orders) is not hereditary, but is bestowed upon him by the sovereign for his lifetime. He may also be a *Knight Bachelor* which means that he is not a member of any of the seven orders. On an envelope a Knight is addressed as "Sir John Smith." Letters are not put after his name unless he is a Knight of the Order of the Garter (K.G.). Those receiving this order are almost certain to be peers as well. Scottish peers have the corresponding Order of the Thistle (K.T.), and Irish peers the corresponding Order of St. Patrick (K.P.). Only on business or professional communications are letters put after the names of Knights who are members of the other orders. You can always look up Knights in the reference books available in public libraries if you are not sure to which order they belong. The wife of a Knight is plain "Lady Smith" and is addressed as such on the envelope, in the body of the letter and in conversation. If a wife is an "Hon." in her own right, she is addressed as "The Hon. Lady Smith" on the envelope.

The Church

An Archbishop is addressed in conversation both on social and on formal occasions as "Your Grace," and in social letters as "My dear Archbishop."

should begin "Your Grace" or "My Lord Archbishop."
An envelope is addressed to "His Grace, the Lord Archbishop of . . . ." His wife is "Mrs. Smith" on all occasions.

A Bishop is addressed socially as "My Lord," although
it is correct for a man to address him as "Sir." Those
who know him well would call him "Bishop." A business letter
would begin "My Lord Bishop" and a social letter "My
dear Lord Bishop," or for those who know him well
"Dear Bishop." Envelopes are addressed: "The Right
Rev. The Lord Bishop of. . . ."

Scottish Bishops are addressed by their names, not by
the names of their diocese: "The Right Rev. Bishop
Macgregor." The Primus is addressed on an envelope as
"The Most Rev. Primus."

A Dean is addressed on the envelope as "The Very
Reverend, the Dean of . . ." and in conversation as
"Mr. Dean," in a letter as "Dear Dean" or "Dear Mr.
Dean."

An Archdeacon is addressed on the envelope as "The
Venerable, The Archdeacon of . . .", in conversation as
"Mr. Archdeacon" and in letters as "Dear Archdeacon"
or "Dear Mr. Archdeacon."

A Canon is addressed as "The Reverend Canon John
Fisher" on the envelope. In conversation he is "Canon
Fisher" and in a letter "Dear Canon."

Clergymen of all denominations are addressed on the
envelope as "The Rev. John Smith," except for Rabbis
who are addressed as "Rabbi J. Cohen" or "Rabbi Dr." In

conversation and in a letter most clergymen and non-conformist ministers are addressed as "Mr. Smith." Roman Catholic priests and some Anglican priests are addressed as "Father Smith." A Rabbi is addressed in conversation and in a letter as "Rabbi Cohen" or, if he is a doctor, as "Dr. Cohen."

The Moderator of the Church of Scotland during his year of office should be addressed on the envelope as "The Right Rev. The Moderator of the General Assembly of the Church of Scotland." In conversation and in a letter he is addressed as "Moderator," or by his name, "Mr. Macgregor" or "Dr. Macgregor."

A Cardinal is addressed on the envelope as "His Eminence John, Cardinal Smith", and in the letter or in conversation as "Your Eminence".

The Law

The Lord Chancellor, who is a Baron and addressed socially as such, is always addressed on envelopes as "The Right Hon. The Lord High Chancellor." This also applies to the Lord Chief Justice and the Master of the Rolls.

Judges are addressed socially by their rank, either "Lord . . ." or "Sir John Smith." A Judge of Appeal is addressed on an envelope as "The Right Hon. The Lord Justice Smith," and on the bench as "My Lord." A Judge of the High Court is officially addressed as "The Hon. Mr. Justice Smith." On the bench he is "My Lord." A Judge of the County Court is addressed on an envelope as "His Honour Judge Smith," and on the bench as "Your Honour."

Queen's Counsel are addressed according to their rank, but always with the letters Q.C. after their names.

Justices of the Peace are addressed on the bench as "Your Worship," otherwise by their rank, and on business and professional envelopes by adding J.P. after their names, e.g. "James Jones Esq., J.P."

Mayors

The chief magistrates of certain cities in England, Ireland and Australia are *Lord Mayors* and addressed on envelopes as "The Right Worshipful, the Lord Mayor of . . .", but the Lord Mayors of London, York, Belfast, Sydney, Melbourne, Adelaide, Perth, Brisbane and Hobart are addressed as "The Right Hon. The Lord Mayor of. . . ." On official occasions a Lord Mayor is addressed as "My Lord" and his wife is addressed as the "Lady Mayoress". Socially they are addressed according to their rank. Other mayors are addressed on the envelope as "The Right Worshipful The Mayor of . . .", in official letters as "Sir" or "Madam," and socially according to their rank. In speech on official occasions they are addressed as "Your Worship" or "Mr. Mayor" or "Madam Mayor."

In Scotland the Lord Provost corresponds to a Lord Mayor, and the Lord Provosts of Edinburgh and Glasgow are addressed on envelopes as "The Right Hon. The Lord Provost of . . . ." Those of Dundee, Aberdeen, Elgin and Perth are addressed as "The Lord Provost of. . . ." Their wives are addressed as "Mrs. MacGregor" and do not share their titles. Other Scottish towns have Provosts which correspond to mayors in England. They are addressed as "The Provost of. . . ."

Government

The Prime Minister and Cabinet Ministers are addressed as "The Right Hon. John Smith M.P.," and in speech by their rank. The courtesy title of "Right Hon." is accorded to Privy Councillors and they retain this for life. Wives do not share the title. The letters P.C. are not put after a name when "The Right Hon." is used.

All members of Parliament are entitled to have the letters M.P. after their name. They are addressed on envelopes as "John Smith Esq., M.P.," and on official letters as "The Right Hon. John Smith, M.P."

Diplomacy

An Ambassador is addressed on an envelope as "His Excellency Sir John Smith, H.B.M.'s (Her Britannic Majesty's) Embassy, Lisbon", and a *Foreign Ambassador* as "His Excellency M. Marchand, The French Ambassador" or "His Excellency The French Ambassador." On formal occasions they are addressed in conversation as "Your Excellency" and so are their wives. Socially they are addressed according to their rank. All foreign diplomats are addressed with the French prefix "Monsieur" or "Madame," whatever their nationality.

General Forms of Address

Surgeons are always addressed in conversation as "Mr. Smith," not "Dr. Smith." On the envelope they are "John Smith Esq., F.R.C.S."

Letters to a local council should be addressed to "The Clerk of the Council." Letters of a general nature concerning the business of a town or a city should be addressed to "The Town Clerk." Letters to societies or clubs should be addressed to "The Secretary."

4

CONVERSATION

Since talking is the main form of communication between human beings, it is sad that so many should find it difficult. If you sit down and think about it, most talk at home, in the office and among close friends is disconnected and *not* conversation. Conversation is an interchange of thought and involves a certain unselfish element of interest shown primarily in the other person and, strange as it may sound, in the subject. Many people find it difficult to stick to the subject under discussion, and wander away without realising that this is discourteous and may sound off-hand.

If maintaining a conversation bothers you, start right from the bottom. Smile as much as you feel able to! At least it invites others to talk to you and lessens your vulnerability as someone who looks shy and gauche. Look at the person with whom you are engaged in conversation, not at your feet, his ears or other and perhaps more interesting people who are coming into the room. This is death to any conversation as well as extremely discourteous—a habit which you will observe far too often at many parties, especially among those who like to style themselves "The Upper Classes"!

Feeling tongue-tied arises from fear of making a fool of oneself or not seeming interesting enough. One of the most attractive things is someone who is interested in *you*. Think of this the other way around when you are talking to anybody, even someone you think is terribly important. He is also human. Asking questions is always a good way to keep talk flowing, but not the kind of staccato inquisitive questioning which smacks of an interview. Ask his opinion of an event which has happened recently, the political situation or perhaps a general problem or subject of public interest. Most people love being asked their opinions, and you need not get on to personal ground until the conversation has been flowing for some time.

Another ingredient which feeds impromptu conversation is having *something* to talk about. This does not mean you have to be an expert on bees or comparative religions, but it does mean that you should read at least one newspaper with care every day (or at least on the day when you know you will have to make small talk). This provides a foundation, for a good talker depends a great deal upon being interested in what goes on around him, and lively minds pick up knowledge from obvious sources such as books, newspapers, films, magazines and television.

Do not talk about yourself constantly. This is a good rule with strangers. They are probably feeling as shy and gauche as you. Learn to listen. This is harder than you might suppose; for it does not mean nodding every two minutes and saying "Yes," which is thought to be the answer to good conversation by some misguided women who have heard that men like to be listened to! It means trying to grasp what the other is saying, and asking intelligent questions or giving your opinion or experience on a particular point. A conversation is like a game of tennis. It involves hitting the ball to and fro, not hanging on to your own subject like grim death or letting the other person do all the hard work.

Do not think that "talking shop" must not be indulged

in on social occasions, for people usually talk best upon a subject they know well. Be careful to gauge the knowledge and interest of your partner in such a conversation. If your kind of shop and his coincide, breathe a sigh of relief and fire away. If it is obviously an effort to keep up, then try a more general topic. The secret of a good conversation is a little clever scouting at the beginning and a smiling, interested approach.

Cocktail Party Conversation

Introductions are often made with little thought and care. Two people are plonked in front of one another, their names barely whispered and no point of contact is established which might spark off the first few minutes of conversation. During that agonising first minute look at the other and smile. There is bound to be *some* chemical reaction. The very effort of trying to be pleasant is most attractive. You might say, "Before I start pouring out my life history, do tell me who you are. I'm Mary Bloggs and I'm an old schoolfriend of Jane's. We've known one another for years." At least this gives your partner a chance of saying either what he does or if he too has known the Bloggs' for some time. It is quite incorrect and very gauche to start with a blatant "What do you do?" or "Tell me about yourself." One is tempted to say "Well, I was born in Java one bright May morning," and go on from there. If *only* one had the courage, cocktail parties might be more amusing.

There is a conversational "no man's land" when the person opposite you seems to be made of granite, and you do not appear to be getting any reaction. "Could you top me up with a little more tonic? My drink is far too strong and that makes me talk too much." This gives him something to *do* and a minute or so to talk of

39

something essentially practical. It is an opening. It is also the woman's social duty to start conversations and to set the tone and subject. Another opening gambit is to tell your partner about an argument you may have had on a general subject (not a personal one), and to ask his opinion. Never start going through a list of people you both might know. This is the height of bad manners and most embarrassing if he knows none of them. It is perfectly correct to ask, however, if you really think there is someone you both might know who is related to the subject under discussion.

Dinner Party Conversation

Conversation at dinner parties depends largely upon a good hostess who has chosen her guests with an eye on the interest they may evoke in one another. A warm welcome and thoughtful introductions will put guests at ease right at the beginning.

Some hostesses like to leave guests standing for drinks before dinner. Others ask their guests to be seated, but a hostess should always seat her guests carefully, and not leave them to find a seat beside another guest to whom they have not been introduced properly.

At the dinner table the host and hostess should start conversation rolling with general remarks, or perhaps by mentioning a subject which they know would probably interest several of the guests. A good hostess should always be watchful and see that no one is left out of a conversation. If this is the case, she should immediately bring that guest into her little circle of talk.

A really courteous guest will take special care to talk to those on his right *and* his left, and not to sink into what might be a private conversation all evening with the person who interests him most. This is an insult to the hostess.

A good hostess sees that everyone enjoys himself and she should talk with every single guest, even though she may find herself more involved with one or two in the course of the evening.

No one should deliver a lecture on his favourite subject or wax violent over an argument, and no one should just sit there and eat as if food were the only important source of pleasure. A dinner party is a social game and the stakes are friendship and social intercourse.

Difficult Topics

It is not always true to say that intelligent people can talk about anything without quarrelling. They *can*, but often they do not. A good hostess should never allow any shadow of disagreement which threatens to become unpleasant to gather upon her table. If guests are old friends who wrangle good naturedly and the subject is of great interest to everyone, then she can let it be, but when strangers are present the hostess must watch for remarks or subjects which might cause offence. She must never let any guest at her table feel hurt or badly treated.

If you know that one guest is a dyed-in-the-wool party man who is intolerant into the bargain, do not invite him with his opposite number (your dinner party is not a television platform), unless you are sure they will both like and be interested in one another.

Religion is a subject to be treated with care. If a guest inadvertently makes a remark which is detrimental to the religion of another guest, the hostess should immediately make a remark in favour of that religion without causing anyone embarrassment. Alternatively she may try to change the subject by saying, "This is dangerous ground, and I'm much too fond of everyone at this table to allow it to develop." Most people will take the hint.

A guest is sacred in your house and should be protected from offence or attack.

Changing a conversation should not be a snap thing after an awkward silence. The host or hostess should refer to the difficult subject and say, "Oh dear, this is a tricky question. Don't let's get into the situation of a man I once knew who leant across the table and gave his tormentor a box on the ear because he was goaded beyond endurance." Or the hostess can say, "All my energy has gone into the pudding. I just can't face an intellectual battle at this time of evening. You're all so clever that you won't appreciate the food." Any guest with half an inch of common sense should take up such an opening with a humorous remark or a change of topic. It is a matter of careful transition, not abrupt change of gear.

General Conversational Rules at Dinner

1. *No one should ever discuss mutual friends to their disadvantage* or indulge in gossip which might upset anyone present. This is the height of bad form.

2. It is no longer considered bad manners to *congratulate a hostess upon the food*. Today, most of them do the cooking themselves and go to a good deal of trouble. It is almost discourteous not to make some compliment to the hostess or to tell her, at the same time, how well she is looking or how attractive is her house. A compliment, unless it is laid on with a trowel, is a delightful and a fairly essential ingredient for a good dinner party.

3. *Husbands and wives should never allow any shadow of a bicker to arise before guests*. Nor should they raise a point of disagreement between them and ask a guest to

42

give an opinion. Even if longing to put him right over a certain point, a hostess should never contradict or show up her husband as being in the wrong.

4. *During a sudden lull,* the best way to start conversation spinning is to offer more wine, or to pretend suddenly to remember some point you wished to ask a guest, which might also be of general interest. When everyone is talking again, the hostess can turn to a guest to whom she had not been talking prior to the lull.

5. *At public functions* you may find yourself talking to a stranger and you have not the faintest idea who he is. Give him a charming smile and ask him his particular interest in this function. Tell him yours and say who you are. It is quite extraordinary how a show of interest brings others to life. At a public dinner you should always talk to guests on either side of you.

6. *Children or teenagers included in a dinner or luncheon party* should listen and join in the conversation from time to time, or if addressed. The French manage a mixture of age groups at meals most beautifully. This is because the young do not *take over*, and while they are included in conversations they are not pandered to. Admittedly, it may be boring for the young who prefer their own age group, but it is by listening to older and perhaps cleverer people that we learn the art of conversation; therefore it is sad to eliminate the young from all social intercourse and very foolish of them to consider any party boring unless they are making themselves felt. It is up to parents to be firm and explain the etiquette of a dinner party to their children.

5

INTRODUCTIONS

Good introductions made with charm and tact are among the best ways to earn a reputation as a man or woman of courtesy, a host and hostess to whose house it is always a pleasure to be invited. Far too many hosts and hostesses lose their heads. The fact that today we meet more people and are more casual in our relationships means that we have to take extra care to make introductions properly. Many hostesses never make any at all, especially at large parties. This is one of the worst features of the English social scene at the moment and guaranteed to make strangers feel utterly miserable. A party is *your* party to which you ask those you like, or find interesting, to meet one another. You are supposed to have selected them with care. At least, this is what a party is meant to be; not free drinks in a private home.

Never take it for granted that even great friends will make their way happily around a group of strangers unless properly introduced.

A Gentleman should always be introduced to a Lady regardless of age or rank, except when introducing people to royalty. You can either say, "May I introduce Mr. Smith?" or "Mrs. Jones: Mr. Smith." Among the same sex, a younger person is introduced to an older one; an unmarried woman to a married one and the untitled are introduced to the titled.

Should you bring a stranger with you to a party (having previously asked your hostess for permission), you introduce him to your hostess right at the beginning after your own greeting, and leave *her* to introduce him to her other guests.

If a woman is married she introduces her mother as "My mother, Mrs. Brown" or her sister as "My sister, Mary Brown." A man or an unmarried woman will introduce parents as "My father," "My mother" or "My sister, Jane," unless the mother and sister have other names through marriage.

You never introduce your wife as "Mrs. Jones" or your husband as "Mr. Jones," but as "My wife, Mary"— or simply "My wife" and "My husband."

Among younger people introductions are becoming less formal, and "John Smith: Mary Jones" instead of "This is John Smith: Mary Jones" is perfectly correct.

Your vicar may be introduced as "This is our vicar, Mr. Green," or simply as "Mr. Green" and, in the case of a Roman Catholic priest, "I'd like you to meet Father Smith, our parish priest."

A man always rises from his seat when introduced to a woman and usually when introduced to another man. A young woman should rise for an older woman. A woman need never rise when a man is introduced to her, unless he is a clergyman or someone much older or someone to whom she feels she owes special respect. A hostess should rise to greet any guest, man or woman. A husband who is the host should rise when his wife enters to greet her guests.

If you forget the name of someone you are introducing at a large party, do not hum and haw or not mention his name at all; laugh and say "How stupid of me, but I have a mental blank whenever there are a great many people around me." He will then murmur his name and cannot possibly be offended.

The Question of Shaking Hands upon introduction needs a little discussion. Some time ago all a woman was expected to do when someone was introduced to her was to smile, incline her head and murmur "How do you do?" presumably a left-over from the days of bowing and curtsying. Although it is still perfectly correct, this little nod today looks condescending and unfriendly, unless the woman is introduced to a group of people and cannot possibly shake hands with them all.

However, it is always up to the woman to offer her hand first. Should a man offer his hand she must always shake it. Not to do this is a studied insult on any occasion.

A hostess should always shake hands with each of her guests. When one person is introduced to another they should both murmur, "How do you do?"; never "Pleased to meet you" or "Hi" or "Hallo."

You do not shake hands when introduced to another person in the street.

Children should be taught to shake hands with guests when they enter a room to be introduced. Nor is it old-fashioned for very small girls to be taught to curtsy, especially if they live in a non-Bohemian home, where there is still some drawing-room atmosphere.

Chance Meetings in the Street. Usually friends nod to one another and smile. A man raises his hat to a woman if she acknowledges him, and a quick "Good morning" may be exchanged. Men do not greet women unless a woman acknowledges them first. Should you wish to stop and say something to an acquaintance and you have someone with you, you *must* introduce him briefly and then go on with what you have to say. This does not mean your friend has to join in the conversation, but it is rude and hurtful to leave him or her standing beside you while you chat on. (In the old days the friend, if a man, was supposed to walk on while you talked, but this is impractical in a crowded street and a rather unnecessary insistence upon the strict laws of etiquette.)

Anyone with whom you walk and talk should be good enough to introduce to another, but any communication in the street should be brief.

Introductions in Theatre or Restaurant. Nothing is more calculated to arousing feelings of sourness in your companion, than for you to spot another friend behind you in the theatre and to turn round and gossip for some minutes without introducing him. It is tantamount to saying that he or she is not good enough to be introduced. Make a brief exchange of names.

If you are with a group of people in a restaurant or theatre foyer, it is impolite to leave them to go and greet someone else, unless you bring him into the group and introduce him. If you feel you cannot do this, acknowledge the friend with a smile and a brief "Hallo".

Never leave a single guest to go over to talk to another friend across a foyer, even if you excuse yourself first. If you really must talk, take your companion with you, make the introductions and have a brief conversation. Your first social duty is to those you are with.

Introductions in the Office should be conducted as in social life, men being introduced to women unless a new woman employee is being introduced to the boss. An immediate superior should always take a new employee round to all those with whom he will be dealing and introduce him. Nothing is more miserable than to be left in an office not knowing who is who.

Introducing Yourself. You may well hope that this occasion won't arise too often, but sometimes it is inevitable at public functions, business conferences and at those dreadful overcrowded cocktail parties where the hostess is nowhere to be seen and the guests are left to sink or swim.

If, at a party, you cannot find your hostess, it is correct to go up to a group of likely-looking people (not a couple deeply embedded in fascinating conversation) and say, "May I introduce myself? I am at a loss because I simply can't find my hostess." Say who you are, and most nice people will immediately rise to the occasion and do their best to make you feel welcome, fetch your hostess or introduce you to others.

Do as you would be done by, and if at a party you see some poor creature wandering about looking lost, go and introduce yourself, after asking if he or she is looking for someone in particular. Say "I am Mary Smith, do come and meet my husband and tell me your name." This is one of the most disarming of American party habits (and should not be confounded with breaking in upon other people's conversation, merely because a man happens to like the look of a girl!)

The old idea that English people never talk unless formally introduced is dead as a dodo in modern society. This is especially so today when we all go to functions and business conferences where it is quite likely that we may know no one there. It is foolish and miserable to sit in a corner like a violet in a field. No one can possibly be offended if you introduce yourself courteously, saying you would like to talk.

A woman taking pity on a man may find this a little more difficult, but she can go up to him and ask if he would like to join the group she is with. She should ask his name and introduce him to the others. Remember that nothing is rude or forward if said with a smile at an opportune moment, in a dignified and charming manner.

A Business Telephone Call to a Private Home may mean you will have to introduce yourself to your colleague's wife if she answers the telephone. Say who you are and ask her if she would take a message or ask her husband to call you back. Thank her for doing this. A private home should never be approached as if it were an office, or a wife as if she were a secretary.

Mind How You Say It

There are certain ways of expressing yourself which are considered the correct ways if you wish to be thought equal with those on the highest social levels. There are certain words considered correct and others considered "common." There is no logical basis for this—it has developed through custom. There is a definite social distinction between people who express themselves in a manner considered to be correct and those who do not, but use the following rules as you think fit.

1. Never say "Pardon," but "I beg your pardon" or "Excuse me."
2. Ask for the "lavatory," or the "loo" if you are young, but not the "toilet" or the "W.C." Ask for the "ladies' cloakroom" in public places.
3. Refer to a woman as a "woman" or a "girl," not as a "lady," unless you are talking to a waiter

and saying, for instance, "Would you fetch the lady's coat?"

Never say "My lady friend" or "My gentleman friend," but "A friend" or "A girl I know" or "A man I know."

4. Never refer to your wife as "The wife" or "Mrs. Smith," but "My wife."

5. Call a living-room a "sitting-room" or a "drawing-room," but never a "lounge." The word "lounge" is only used in a hotel or on board ship.

6. Talk about a "table napkin" or "napkin," not a "serviette."

7. Never refer to a magazine as a "book." A book is a "book" and a magazine is a "magazine."

8. Say that you are going "riding," not "horse riding."

9. After the meat course you will have a "pudding," not a "sweet." "Dessert" is nuts and fruit.

10. Offer your guests "vegetables," but not "greens."

11. Do not repeat people's names every five minutes in conversation. Say "Yes," or "No," or "I must tell you;" not "Yes, Mrs. Smith," "No, Mrs. Smith," "I must tell you, Mrs. Smith."

12. Avoid mannerisms such as "Fancy that!" or "My word!" or "Did you ever?"

6

ETIQUETTE IN A MODERN WORLD

On the Telephone

In a fast-moving world the telephone is an important means of communication and, considering how much business as well as "socialising" is carried on via the telephone, it is surprising how many people still forget the simplest rules for good telephone manners, although they may be utterly delightful to *meet*. Secretaries in offices, assistants in shops and that hardy race of women who make all their complaints on the telephone seem to think that, because the other person cannot see them, they can be as rude and abrupt as they like.

Those whose job it is to answer calls in business are like public relations officers. They are the initial contact with the outside world—they present the "public image" of their firm, and many a new contract may stand or fall according to their manner of dealing with a call. Terrible mistakes can be made on the telephone, merely because it is an impersonal instrument. Extra care should be taken, then, especially if you do not know the person at the other end of the line.

Timbre of Voice Matters. Never shout. Do not talk too fast. A low voice is more attractive and carries better. Try to say the person's name at least *once* in the course of the conversation. It is much nicer to hear, "Yes, Mrs. Brown, I know exactly what you want. I'll put you through to Mr. Jones who will help you." than, "Yes, I'll put you through to Mr. Jones." There is something very attractive about the sound of one's name when it is repeated by a stranger across the wires. It means you become a person to him, not just a voice out of nowhere, and the contact is less impersonal. The name should not, of course, be repeated with every breath. This is one of the points of etiquette which is happily changing. It used to be said that using a person's name in conversation was "not done." Psychologically, this is cold and unfriendly and times are changing—for the better in many ways.

Answering Calls at Home. State your number—do not just say "Hallo." This prevents cross talk about wrong numbers. If you are a wife receiving a business call for your husband, sound efficient and friendly, take down any message and say when he will be home or where he can be contacted. Try not to sound inquisitive or bored by the whole thing. If you have kept someone waiting, apologise.

Say Who You Are. In a private call say "This is Mary Smith," and at business "This is Mrs. Smith" or "This is Mr. Green's assistant," or your department and then your name.

If you have dialled a Wrong Number say "I'm afraid I dialled the wrong number. I'm sorry." This is a courtesy that may get you nowhere, but it is satisfying to the inner woman (or man), and you can say to yourself "I am a lady. I know how to behave." All this is a far greater sign of good breeding than changing for dinner in the jungle; also far more reasonable behaviour.

If a Conversation is getting too long and you simply

must end it, try to do so with charm. "Goodness, how time flies when I'm talking to you. I must deal with the dinner," or "fly to an appointment." A little subtle flattery makes an ending less abrupt.

If Someone Rings you in the Middle of a Party and he or she is the kind who chats on *ad infinitum*, say right at the beginning that you are having a party and cannot stay long. Offer to call back in the morning if there is a matter to be discussed. Do not get into a panic, sound icy because your nerves are jittery, then say you must go. Say you would rather call back at leisure because you want to "talk properly," thank your caller and say good night.

Standing Up for Others
When is it necessary? (*See page* 45 re Standing up for Introductions). A man should always stand up when a woman enters the room, unless he is her boss in the office. Husbands should stand up for their wives in front of guests. Children and young people should stand up when their parents' guests enter the room. Unless your boss is popping into your office all day, it is polite to stand up when he or she calls in to see you. Standing up for older people in tubes or on buses is a courtesy, and whatever a man's views about female emancipation it is courteous for him to stand up when a woman, his age or older, stands beside him in a public conveyance.

Flat-sharing
Sharing flats is becoming more common every day, when young people leave home fairly soon after their schooldays to set up a flat with two or three others. It is good practice in how to get on with others, in learning

the value of money and preparing to run one's own home (if the flat-sharers are all girls). If they are young men, then it provides an excellent chance of learning just how exacting and sometimes tiresome a woman's chores can be!

It is important to decide how expenses are to be shared right at the very beginning and to stick to the decision. One person at a time should take on the responsibility of collecting money for rent, gas, electricity, etc. The best way to share food bills is for everyone to put, say, £1 in the "kitty" each week for basics such as milk, bread, coffee, tea, salt, butter, marmalade, and to pay individually for his or her own parties and evening meals. But this has to be worked out according to whether the flat-sharers are people who go out a great deal or stay in every night. Careless treatment of finances can lead to more quarrels, bitterness and broken friendships than almost anything else.

Each one should have his or her own cupboard or half cupboard, drawers and shelf in the kitchen for individual luxuries and food.

Definite arrangements should be made about who is to do the cleaning or how to share it. It does not matter how this is worked out, either daily, weekly or by rota, but a fair division must be made or someone will soon be feeling "put upon."

One can go on for ever about how to share flats happily, but the basis is equal sharing in as many respects as possible, even if this means making lists and sticking them up in the kitchen. It is much better to have chores cut and dried than to wonder vaguely who should be doing what.

Living in a community, however small, needs a certain amount of unselfishness. Do not hog the living-room every night to chat with your guests. Ask the others if it is convenient to them. Be tactful about the personal relationships of the others. If someone wants to talk with a friend, stay in your bedroom that evening or go out to the cinema. Mutual consideration in all things is the key to happy flat-sharing.

The Girl Who Lives Alone

Today this need cause no raising of eyebrows providing the girl is not too young, that her parents approve and that she is ordinarily sensible. It is wise for her not to put her Christian name in the telephone book, merely her initials before her surname, as otherwise she may receive tiresome calls.

If you do not want a man who has taken you out to come in for a drink late at night, you are perfectly correct in thanking him at the front door and going upstairs alone. No man has the right to expect to be asked in by a single girl, late at night. But do so without hurting his pride or causing embarrassment to both of you. Say while you are on the way home that you are tired and intend to be asleep within the half hour. Anyway, make your point *before* you arrive on the doorstep so that you do not have to be embarrassed, or give in in spite of yourself when you are opening the door.

If he insists upon coming in, say firmly but nicely that you are tired and would he mind letting you go as soon as you arrive home. (Never say "I *never* have men in my flat," because it is probably not true and besides it is guaranteed to annoy, upset him or merely make him decide that this is the end of you!)

If you have friends in to a dinner party or drinks and one of the men stays on, showing no sign of getting up to go, you are perfectly entitled to say cheerfully that it is getting late and you must get to bed, because you have to be up early in the morning, and that he ought to be going home too. (Something which it is difficult to say to a group of guests, but perfectly permissible to a single man.)

Etiquette for Smokers

This consists of a series of short "do's" and "dont's", not mere suggestions.

1. Do not smoke at a dinner party unless your host or hostess says that guests may smoke. Do not even ask for permission. It is not a habit to be fostered at any meal, but in other people's houses it is unforgivable unless the hostess gives her permission.
2. A man should always ask a woman's permission to smoke when he is with her or sitting talking to her in a drawing-room.
3. Do not puff cigarette smoke into other people's faces and always offer to put out a cigarette if it appears to be causing distress.
4. Never smoke in the street or enter someone else's house smoking a cigarette.
5. Never smoke at an interview, unless you are offered a cigarette.
6. Do not smoke in any place where it might be unwelcome, such as in a hospital, school or sickroom.
7. Pipes should never be smoked at any kind of formal dinner, luncheon or cocktail party.
8. If you can bear it, try not to smoke in theatres or cinemas as this often distresses others, particularly in a close atmosphere.

Etiquette and Animals

As we all live in a pretty tight community, especially in towns, a dog should be trained to obey you promptly and not to annoy others. It should never be allowed to make messes on the pavement, but should be taken to the kerbside. Never take a dog to someone else's house unless you have warned them beforehand and asked if it is convenient. If you have a variety of animals at home, keep them out of the way of guests. Nothing is more disconcerting than to find a hamster poking about on the sofa, or being unable to sit down because all the chairs are filled with dogs and cats.

Choosing a School for Your Child

If you are unsure about where to send your child, go and visit the local education officer and discuss the various schools in your district. Should you want a private school, write to and then visit any of the educational agencies which exist in most large towns. Most public schools require a child to be entered at birth. You should write to the headmaster or headmistress asking if you may visit the school to discuss your child, the kind of education you want, fees, health, etc. Some people enter their child for two or three schools just to make sure of obtaining a place for him.

It is perfectly correct to ask if you may visit the school more than once, especially when you can see the other children at play or engaged in various activities. The headmaster or headmistress may ask for references, both social and business. You can give the names of your bank manager, solicitor, doctor, parish priest and any personal friends you have known for a long time, particularly those who may have some connection with the school.

57

Joining a Club

For a man a club can be an important business asset, where he can entertain business acquaintances and colleagues, as well as personal friends, to meals and drinks. Women who live in the country and rarely come to town may find a ladies' club a useful place in which to stay and entertain friends.

At most clubs you cannot propose yourself for membership but must be proposed by a friend who is already a member, although you must not ask him outright unless he is a great personal friend or a relation. A club is a home from home and usually fairly exclusive to certain kinds of people, who may vary from members of the services (or ex-members) to certain professions, or those with special interests such as sport or particular political affiliations.

Your friend will propose you and this proposal will be seconded by another member of the club. It is then considered by the membership committee.

There are certain clubs where you can apply for membership by writing to the Secretary. You will usually have to be proposed and introduced by another member who, if he will sponsor you, will take it upon himself to find another sponsor. The Secretary will send you an application form which will, in due course, be put before the club committee. The Secretary will then let you know if you have been elected and you will be asked to send your subscription.

The rules of club behaviour are fairly stringent. All dues or subscriptions must be paid promptly. This is a point of honour. Complaints about food, service and so on are made to the Secretary in writing.

As a club is meant to be a home from home, it is understood that members will not entertain anyone who does not fit into the atmosphere of the club.

Bills are often paid at the end of the month and a bill for a meal may be signed. Servants are not usually tipped, except at Christmas when a list is put out for this purpose, and you fill in the amount you wish to give.

If you are a guest at a friend's club, you meet him or wait for him in the hall after having told the porter the name of your host. You do not wander about the club or go up to any of the rooms. You never tip servants or offer to pay for a drink in a friend's club, even if there is a bar. You behave with your host as you would in his own home.

Visiting the Sick

Visiting the sick may be one of the major works of mercy, but it can also be one of the most tiresome, not only for the patient concerned but also for the professional staff in charge of the wards.

For those who have trekked miles or waited ages to see a friend or relation it is very difficult to remember that often it tires very ill people, and even convalescents, to have visitors who stay too long. The pleasure of considerate and thoughtful friends is ruined when they stay and stay, chat too loudly, talk to one another across the bed or continually ask questions. An ill person is using up all his reserves of both physical and mental energy in order to get better, and to give deep attention to a problem or dish out information can drain him completely. If you really want to do good by taking the trouble to visit sick people, be sure that you think first about their condition. Most ill people like being talked to lightly, but cannot cope with solving problems or raking up old worries.

If you find there are several others round the bed (because there is no hospital rule about one or two visitors at a time), smile and greet your sick friend and ask if he would prefer you to go outside for a few minutes while he talks to the others. This is not only a very thoughtful and courteous act, but it is sometimes essential to prevent the patient's getting over-excited and tired. A naturally kind person, however ill, will get confused and worried if he feels he cannot talk to all his visitors, and there are too many people gathered around at the same time with him as the focal point. The strain is terrific.

Do not make a noise outside the ward. If you arrive early do not try to get in before the others, or stay after the bell has gone for visitors to leave, with the excuse that you are a close relation. Every hospital staff member would like patients to see visitors as often as is good for them, but the daily administration of a ward is impossible without fairly strict rules. (This also applies to visiting friends in private rooms, where the administration is as difficult as in public wards and perhaps even more so.)

Do not ask any nurse who happens to be at hand for a long description of the patient's condition. Such questions should be addressed only to the sister or the doctor, and only if the patient is a near relation.

If you are bringing any kind of food as a present, try to find out from the sister if it is suitable for the patient at this particular time.

If it is at all possible for you to telephone a sick person, do tell him when you propose to visit and ask if it is convenient or whether there are other visitors coming at that time.

Many people who have spent some time in hospital complain that they receive all their visitors, presents, flowers and inquiries right at the beginning, and are left almost in penal solitude for the rest of their stay. Somehow, visitors feel they have done their duty if they go at the beginning. But it is not only at the onset of hospitalisation (when all is rather new and perhaps the patient still feels pretty ghastly) that visitors are most welcome. During the convalescent period he feels bored and terribly cut off from his friends and the outside world, which appears to be managing perfectly well without him. This is the time when ill persons need cheering up, moral support, gossip and friendship.

That Embarrassing Moment

It happens to all of us—the moment when we wish the earth would open up and swallow us. It may happen often or rarely but be prepared for it.

1. You break something in a friend's house. Apologise, but do not make a fuss about it or go on referring to it all evening. Never offer to pay for it on the spot. Your hostess will feel bound to refuse. If it is something you can easily replace, buy it within the next few days and have it sent with a note of apology. If it is not, and it may be dear to your poor hostess, a bunch of flowers sent the following day or a gift for the house accompanied by a note will show that you are really sorry and wish to make amends.

2. Giving References. If someone asks you to give a reference and you are not at all keen but you do not like to refuse, make the reference as brief and non-committal as you can. There is *something* agreeable to say about most people. To refuse a reference is to gain an enemy for life.

3. Refusing Verbal Invitations. This often happens at other people's parties. Do not lose your head and let yourself and your husband in for something you will

regret. Protect yourself by saying "I would love to. May I telephone you in the morning because I do not have my diary with me?" You can then take down the telephone number. This will give you time to think of an appropriate excuse if you do not want to go.

4. You are short of a knife, spoon or fork at a dinner party. Try to make do with what you have, but if you cannot, ask your hostess quietly for the missing piece of cutlery or ask the servant who hands you a dish.

5. If you are given as a present something you had asked a friend to obtain for you, and you had fully expected to pay for it, just say very courteously and firmly that you simply must pay for it, since you had requested it in the first place. If the donor insists that it is a present, do not go on for ages but be prepared to accept it graciously. To refuse a present, unless it is an obvious bribe, is insulting and hurtful. Never return with another present soon after you have been given one. This is a strict rule of etiquette, as it takes away all the pleasure of giving; it intimates a "tit for tat" basis.

6. If you are out with friends and you are very anxious to go to the lavatory. This is *not* necessarily an embarrassing situation. It is only your attitude which could make it so. Say quietly to your hostess "Do you know where the Ladies' Cloakroom is?" or, if you are with a man, you can ask him to wait for you a few minutes while you go and tidy up. The less fuss, the more ordinary it will seem.

7. If you are greeted as a long lost friend by someone you feel sure you do not know (unless it is a man who appears to be "picking you up," in which case you just walk on and take no notice), let the other person do all the talking. Smile and look friendly, and if he or she realises it is a mistake you can both laugh together. It

is far more likely to be someone who remembers you, although you may have forgotten him. If you are with a friend and have to make introductions, say simply "It's too stupid, but I just can't remember your name." Do not shuffle, look affronted or embarrassed. It may be your husband's boss!

8. If, at a dinner party, another guest makes disparaging remarks about your race or religion it is really up to your hostess to put a stop to this. If she does not, it is kinder to her not to make a fuss but to keep quiet or to say, "You know I am a . . . and I find all this rather hurtful." Never retaliate with anger or by saying something equally unpleasant.

7

APPROACHING THE PROFESSIONS

What is a professional man? Basically, he is someone who professes to be skilled in a certain occupation or vocation, and who strictly adheres to a code of professional rules, usually embodied in statutes. He is registered by his institute or association as having achieved a certain standard in his studies, and any member of a profession who disobeys the professional rules or falls short of a standard of professional behaviour can be struck off the list of registered persons. Alternatively he may be suspended for a time, or indefinitely, from practising his profession.

The professions used to embody those persons practising the law, medicine and divinity as well as the army and the navy. Today they also include architects, accountants and others who belong to a recognised body—and of course the air force.

Chartered Accountants
As with other professions the best way is to obtain an introduction from friends, bank manager, solicitor or inspector of taxes. Otherwise, write to the Institute of Chartered Accountants in England and Wales, Moorgate Place, London, E.C.2. There are separate chartered institutes for Scotland and Ireland (The Institute of Chartered Accountants of Scotland, 27 Queen Street Edinburgh, 2 and The Institute of Chartered Accountants in Ireland, 7 Fitzwilliam Place, Dublin, C.2.) They will

then send you a list of chartered accountants in your area or town but cannot recommend one as this would be unprofessional.

There is a small booklet which outlines the services which chartered accountants can provide called *See a Chartered Accountant*, which can be obtained from the Institute of Chartered Accountants in England and Wales.

It is not always appreciated that whilst no one may describe himself as a solicitor unless he has studied and properly qualified in accordance with the regulations of The Law Society, any member of the public may describe himself as an "accountant." The Companies Act, 1948 went some way towards remedying this anomaly by stating that unless specifically authorised by the Board of Trade, a person shall not be qualified for appointment as auditor of a company, other than an exempt private company, unless "he is a member of a body of accountants established in the United Kingdom and for the time being recognised for this purpose by the Board of Trade." The three chartered institutes and the Association of Certified and Corporate Accountants, 22 Bedford Square, London, W.C.1 have been recognised by the Board of Trade so that their members are qualified to act as auditors of companies. There are also two other United Kingdom bodies of high standing in the limited fields indicated by their names. These are the Institute of Municipal Treasurers and Accountants and the Institute of Cost and Works Accountants.

Advertisements in the press by or circulars from "Accountants" or "Tax Experts" etc., offering their professional services, are therefore issued by unqualified men who are not members of the recognised bodies of accountants.

Doctors

A doctor is approached either through recommendation by friends, in the case of a private practice, or directly by attending his surgery and asking if he will take you on his list of patients. Most National Health Service doctors will only take patients who live within the district they serve, but in case of emergency any doctor can be called upon and, according to the rules of his profession, must attend you. A list of local doctors can be obtained from the Citizens' Advice Bureau and there is sometimes a list displayed in the post office.

If you are on holiday and need medical attention, you can go to any doctor who practises under the National Health Act and be treated by him as a temporary resident. If there is an emergency at home and you cannot contact your own doctor, you can ask any other National Health Service doctor to come to you. But you must be certain that your own doctor is not available.

All practising doctors are registered with the General Medical Council, 44 Hallam Street, London, W.1, which is the body responsible for discipline. Private patients wishing to complain of unprofessional practice should write to the Council. Patients registered with National Health Service doctors should write to their local medical executive councils, and if need be the matter is taken up by the Ministry of Health.

Specialists are usually approached through your own doctor, who will write to make an appointment, although some specialists do see patients direct. The point is that a specialist, in most cases, likes to have some medical information about you and your ailment. Without this he cannot treat you unless he "starts at the beginning."

Changing Your Doctor. Some people think that because they are on the National Health Service they cannot change their doctor and go to another. This is not so. You are as free to choose your doctor as anyone who pays fees. Medical etiquette is such, however, that another doctor cannot treat you unless your original doctor has clearly been told that you are going to another and that he is no longer responsible. A new doctor can refuse to attend you (except in an emergency) until the present one has been notified.

On your medical card there is a paragraph which states "I agree to immediate transfer of this patient. . . ." You can get your doctor to sign this and transfer immediately, taking the card to the new doctor, to whom all your documents should also be forwarded.

On the other hand, if you do not want the embarrassment of facing your doctor and saying you wish to go to another, you can write to your executive council (the address is on the front of your card), saying you wish to change your doctor (you need not give the name of the new doctor) and enclosing your card. They will return it to you with a white card inside. This you send to your new doctor, but there must be a lapse of fourteen days between your notifying the executive council and seeing a new doctor.

Should you wish to visit a consultant for further advice, without necessarily changing your doctor, you can arrange to do this through your doctor, who will give you a letter. He cannot refuse to let you visit any consultant you wish, although he may advise against it.

Solicitors

The best way of approaching a solicitor is to ask friends to recommend a firm of solicitors. You will then write a letter to the firm (solicitors prefer everything in writing), and ask if they will take on your affairs or a particular problem. Most solicitors like a reference, so it is wise to state the name of your bank, the firm for which you work and perhaps your accountants. The solicitor will then ask you to deliver to him all documents pertaining to the affairs or problem in question.

The Citizens' Advice Bureau in your locality will also have a list of solicitors willing to act on a legal aid basis, and appointments can be made for certain days each week.

Any really serious complaint against a solicitor should be sent in writing to the Law Society, 133 Chancery Lane, W.C.2. But this measure should only be taken in exceptional circumstances when a client feels that some dishonest or grossly unprofessional act has taken place.

Barristers can be approached only through a solicitor.

Changing Your Solicitor. The rules for changing your doctor are also applicable here. A personal letter must be written to your solicitor, as your new solicitor will not wish to undertake your work until you have told the present one that you no longer want to use his services.

Architects

The best way to find an architect is to ask your friends and get a personal recommendation. If you cannot do this, write to the Royal Institute of British Architects, 68 Portland Place, London, W.1, asking for a list of architects (if you live in London). If you live elsewhere they will send you the address of your local chapter of the R.I.B.A. who will supply you with a list of architects in your locality. They cannot recommend any particular architect as this would be unprofessional.

No one can call himself an architect unless he is registered as such. There is a small booklet called *Conditions of Engagement and Scale of Professional Charges* which you can obtain from your registered architect, and which states the scale of charges and the arrangements which govern them. There is a definite minimum scale so that no architect can undercut another, but there is no maximum scale.

There is no binding agreement that an architect must finish the job if you are not satisfied with what he is doing, but he will have to be paid according to the amount of work (e.g. drawings, etc.) he may have completed.

8

COMMITTEES[1]

Most people find that, at one time or another, they are
asked to serve on a committee, whether it is concerned
with politics, a school, a hospital management board or
a group of local ladies getting together to organise a
charitable function. Or, if you are particularly interested
in the activities of a certain society and have met one of
the members and expressed this interest, you may be put
up for election. Even if you know no one but still want
to join in some activities where committee membership
is necessary, you can write to the secretary and tell him
or her why you think you might be of use as a member.
Your name will be put before the committee and usually
must be proposed and seconded before you are eventually
asked to "stand." Then your election will be put to the
ballot and members will vote for or against your election.

Voting papers are sent round with the names of intending
new members and their proposers, and although various
societies have their own methods of electing members,
the usual one is by a percentage of votes over a certain
figure. Some societies demand 100% acceptance while
others may require 80%.

If you have been told in a letter that you have been
elected to a committee you should immediately write
back to the Secretary, accepting and saying how pleased
and honoured you are and how you will try to do your

[1] See Phyllis Bentley's book *Committees*, in the Nutshell series.

70

best for the society and help the committee as much as possible.

A committee meeting is run by the Chairman, and a quorum should be present—that is a minimum number of members, according to the constitution of the society—or valid business cannot take place. This protects the society and its members from dictatorship or rule by the minority.

The Chairman usually introduces the subjects to be discussed that day and any speakers, and then asks the Secretary to read the minutes of the last meeting. When this has been done the Chairman asks the members if they agree that he or she should sign the minutes as accurate. Each page of the minutes is then signed by the Chairman if everyone has agreed.

The Chairman then calls each item of the agenda for the day, puts it to the committee for discussion or calls upon any speakers who have previously been asked to talk upon or discuss a point.

Any motions which have to be passed by the committee, that is any course of action which calls for a "yes" or "no," must be proposed, discussed and voted upon. The Chairman organises this procedure.

All remarks are addressed to the Chair, and members must not talk among themselves during a meeting. The Chairman is responsible for the maintenance of order.

The Secretary, or a shorthand typist, will be taking down notes of everything reported, discussed or decided. The agenda for the next meeting may be discussed, or it may have to be compiled by the Secretary, in conjunction with the Chairman, before the next meeting as problems or ideas come up in the period between.

Members may ask that a certain subject be raised at a forthcoming meeting. This should, if possible, be added to the agenda, and must, therefore, be submitted to the Secretary as far in advance of the meeting as possible. The Chairman has to approve the addition of such items to the agenda.

The Chairman then opens the meeting, keeps order throughout the meeting, sums up at the end, and finally dismisses the meeting. A Vice-chairman takes the place of the Chairman if he or she cannot be present.

The Treasurer is responsible for all financial matters concerning the society or organisation. He collects subscriptions, pays accounts and draws up statements of income and expenditure. These are usually read out to the members at the end of the financial year.

The Secretary has the most onerous job of all and is responsible for the running of the society or group. He or she keeps lists of members and their addresses and telephone numbers and deals with applications and resignations. The Secretary deals with all correspondence and sees that the decisions of the committee are put into effect. Other duties include drawing up the agenda and circulating copies to all members before each meeting, also bringing documents concerning the subjects to be discussed at a meeting when and where they may be needed. The Secretary is responsible for the minutes (even if a shorthand typist actually takes the notes) and for the annual report which has to be read out at the Annual General Meeting and adopted by all members, or by an executive committee, if there is one.

9

ENTERTAINING AT HOME

A Well Appointed House

Although your house should reflect your personality above all else, as should the clothes you wear, and no one can dictate to you what goes into your house or on your back, there are a few points which might help those who worry about the impression their homes may give to friends and business acquaintances. If your husband places a great deal of emphasis upon entertaining important colleagues or clients at home, or you entertain people whom you look upon (probably unreasonably) as on a higher social level than yourself, and this matters to you, it is wise:

1. Not to over-furnish to such an extent that no one can move around without knocking things over, or to have so many trinkets lying around that it is impossible to put down a pin upon any surface.

2. To avoid such things as flights of duck upon the wall, plastic or coloured gnomes and animals set out before the front door, chimes instead of a doorbell, or door-plaques which are supposed to be funny, like "Men at Work," or which give the names of rooms.

3. To have plenty of fresh air circulating round the house, without leaving guests in a gale or an icy draught. A close, ill-smelling house is extremely disagreeable. See that rooms are aired after heavy smoking.

4. To take trouble with pretty table settings and to

arrange flowers when guests are expected. This shows a hostess has taken trouble.

5. Never to have cruets on a table, but individual salt cellars and mustard and pepper pots. Pepper mills are used only with smoked salmon or caviar.

6. To have enough ash-trays when guests are expected.

7. To see that guests have a place to hang their outer clothes, or a room where they can leave them on a bed.

8. To see that the bathroom is always left impeccably clean, whenever guests come to the house—and no underwear left hanging to dry or in the washbasin, or overflowing dirty clothes baskets. A clean hand-towel and a new cake of soap should be on the wash-basin, enough lavatory paper on the roll and a box of tissues left open on a chest-of-drawers or dressing-table.

9. Never to let a guest shiver even if you stint yourself on the heating. It is extremely thoughtless and discourteous. Be sensitive to pinched faces and the occasional shiver. Offer to turn on the heat or put more coal on the fire and seat the guest beside it.

10. To remove clothes from the washing line in the garden when guests are expected in the day-time.

Party Principles

Inviting others to your home is the greatest compliment you can pay them. Taking trouble really pays dividends and taking no trouble at all can make a party an embarrassing and unsatisfactory affair. Any party requires planning, proper invitations according to the occasion, a careful choice of people and a hard-working, tactful and unselfish host and hostess.

At a large party it is always a good idea to have several friends you know very well and upon whom you can count to talk and be charming with others. You can ask them to help you in this way and they will feel flattered and "special." No party should be made up of complete strangers to you or to each other.

Never invite too many guests and then retire like a modest violet to let them get on with it. Party-giving is hard work and a good host and hostess should make it their duty to talk to every guest, to introduce properly, to see everyone has enough food and drink and to see that everyone enjoys himself.

Welcoming Guests

It is always a good idea to plan beforehand where women guests are to leave their coats (either in your bedroom or a spare room), and ask the men to leave theirs in a hall or cloakroom. If you have a servant to open the door, she should direct guests to the places where they can leave their things, before she takes them to the room where the party is being held. On formal occasions, guests can be announced by the servant, "Mr. and Mrs. Smith," "Miss Smith and Mr. Jones," and the hostess should always be near the door to welcome them.

If you have no one else to open the door, your husband should take on this duty while you welcome guests in the drawing-room. If the party is a large one, he will tell them where to leave their things and ask them to come into the room as soon as they are ready. But a host or hostess should always be near the door until every guest has arrived so that no one is left anxiously looking for them.

Dinner Parties

Guests should be invited to formal dinner parties about ten to fifteen days beforehand, and not less than five days before an informal dinner. Whether she issues her invitations by letter or by telephone, a hostess should make it quite clear at what time she wishes guests to arrive. "Seven forty-five for eight o'clock" means that she is allowing about a quarter of an hour for drinks. She should also make it quite clear how formal the dinner is to be. "Black tie" means that the men are to wear dinner jackets and the women very formal cocktail dresses. Otherwise, the men will wear dark city suits and the women cocktail dresses. If the hostess says "Oh, don't dress up," the men should still wear dark suits but the women can wear a dark wool dress.

The usual time of a dinner party is 7.45 or 8 o'clock. Most dinner parties today are for six or eight people. The large dinners for twelve to eighteen people are rare because we all have smaller houses and servants are scarcer.

A guest should always answer an invitation immediately, and should never break an engagement lightly. He should also take care to be punctual.

A woman always enters the drawing-room first, followed by her husband. When introductions have been made, the host offers drinks, either sherry, an aperitif or a cocktail. On the whole women should sit down while men remain standing, but there is no hard and fast rule about this. It depends very much on the size of the room and whether people know each other well or not. When guests are strangers to one another they will warm up faster if the women are sitting and talking for the first fifteen minutes and the men are standing and talking.

When the dinner is ready, some fifteen to twenty minutes later, the hostess asks her most important woman guest to come in to dinner. The other women follow and the host after them with the men guests.

A good hostess always plans exactly where everyone

is to sit so that her guests do not hang about like a miniature bus queue while she hums and haws. At large or formal dinners a place name can be put above each cover, and guests (with the help of host and hostess) can find their own seats.

The most important woman sits on the right of the host and the most important man on the right of the hostess.

Table Settings and Decorations. Either a beautiful tablecloth or place mats on a polished table are correct. Napkins must be made of material and not of paper. The cutlery is laid on either side of the plate so that the guest works inwards from the outside. Thus, on the right, is the soup spoon, meat knife and pudding spoon. On the left, starting with the outside, a fork for hors d'œuvre (never a knife as well), meat fork and pudding fork. To place the pudding spoon and fork above the place setting is "nursery," but not incorrect. It is not necessary to provide butter at a dinner party but, if you do, the butter knife goes between the soup spoon and the meat knife. No pudding is ever eaten with a spoon alone, unless it is a cream or ice cream. Then a special small spoon is placed on the inner right-hand side.

Glasses are placed at the top right of each place. These are normally from left to right: water glass, white wine glass and red wine glass. But at most dinner parties, one wine glass, or a water glass and wine glass, are the only glasses laid. If the dinner is very formal, there will be a glass for port on the extreme right. The bread plate goes on the left of the cover with the napkin on top of it.

No tall flowers should ever be placed on a dinner table, forcing guests to crane to speak to one another. Floating flower heads in a shallow bowl look beautiful or simply a couple of silver or bronze animals facing one another in the centre of the table (this was a custom in Georgian times), or a dish of china fruit. It is better to have two sets of salt, pepper and mustard and to place a set at either end of the table than to have only one, which means that guests have to ask for them. At some very grand dinner parties, there is an individual set for each guest but this, for obvious reasons, is rare. It is "not done" to have cruets on a dinner table.

Salad is served after the meat course on special side plates, usually curved like half moons.

If you have someone to Wait at Table, he or she serves soup from a tureen at the sideboard, carries each plate (one at a time) to a guest and serves from the left. Avocado pears, melon or a shrimp cocktail may be placed at each cover beforehand.

Meat and birds should be carved in the kitchen, and it is wise to arrange a large dish with the meat and one vegetable beautifully "laid" out upon it. A second vegetable can be handed around in another dish. It is not necessary to offer second helpings at a formal dinner party. It used never to be done, but today it is entirely up to the hostess.

Guests are usually served with pudding from a bowl. They help themselves and do not have individual bowls placed before them already containing the pudding.

Should dessert be served (fruit and nuts), a fruit plate is put before each guest with a fruit knife and fork already placed upon it, and the dishes are placed upon the table for guests to help themselves.

Finger bowls with water in them are placed on the left of the guest so that fingers can be lightly dabbed and dried on the napkin (but never wiped).

When port and dessert are served, everything else is cleared from the table, including bread plates, salt, pepper and mustard pots, and all cutlery which has not been used. The port is circulated round the table (clockwise from the host's left) and each guest pours out for himself.

A maid or manservant always starts to serve the most important woman guest and then passes to the woman on the left of the host and then to the other guests as they are seated. She returns to serve the host last. The servant will go round with the wine asking each guest very quietly if he or she will have some wine. A guest can refuse.

If there is no Servant, it is wise to start a meal with something cold like melon, avocado, cold soup or pâté, which is already on the table, and to have a cold pudding. This means that the hostess is not always disappearing into the kitchen to see how the food is getting on. The host will have carved the meat in the kitchen or on the sideboard, and the hostess will serve her guests. After each course the host and hostess clear away plates but do not allow guests to get up and help, as this makes any dining-room look like a railway station. The hostess fetches the pudding while her husband places plates before the guests, before she serves it.

If port is being served, the host will put port glasses beside each guest, and after having offered port to the woman on his right he will then pass it round to the guests on his left.

Decanting and Glasses. There are two reasons for decanting wine. (1) To serve wine in a more beautiful receptacle than a bottle. (2) Old wines and vintage port must be decanted through a strainer and poured out very carefully to get rid of the sediment. You never decant champagne or sparkling wine.

There are many glasses on the market, but basically a wine glass should be of not too thick glass. It should be reasonably large and slightly curved towards the top so as to retain the bouquet, and it should never be filled more than half-way.

There is absolutely no need to use the traditional champagne glasses for champagne or the balloon shaped glasses for brandy. Both these wines are drunk by connoisseurs from the tulip-shaped wine-taster's glass which costs very little.

Sherry and liqueurs can be drunk from smaller tulip-shaped glasses, cocktails from wine glasses and long drinks, such as whisky and soda or gin and tonic, from tumblers.

Coffee. To get up or not to get up for coffee is a matter of choice today. Some people (especially if conversation is going well) prefer to remain at table to drink their coffee and only move to another room later on if there is a lull in the talk. Others like to go to the drawing-room, leaving the men behind to drink port or brandy and talk for about fifteen minutes. The hostess gets up to take the women to her bedroom if they wish to tidy up and renew their make-up. She then goes to the drawing-room with the coffee tray laid with coffee cups, sugar crystals and a jug of cream. (If there is a servant, she brings the tray in.) Liqueurs are then offered if port has not been drunk.

The Problem of Leaving. As most people have to go to work the following day, guests should leave a dinner party around 11 to 11.30 p.m. The host may offer whisky and soda and soft drinks around 10.30, and a thoughtful guest will not stay much longer. Staying too long ruins many an excellent dinner party. It is really up to the eldest or most important guest to leave first and the others follow suit.

Cocktail Parties

An invitation for drinks around 6.30 to a dozen or more people constitutes a cocktail party. An "At Home" card is sent out a fortnight before the date of the party, although this is only necessary when the numbers are over twenty. A telephone call is perfectly correct when inviting a small number. Many people find that drinks already poured out into glasses and offered around on trays is the easiest way to see that every guest is quickly served when he enters the room. If you can afford champagne you need have no other kind of drink; otherwise whisky and soda, martinis, sherry, gin and tonic and tomato juice provide a good selection. You can also offer sherry alone, but you must state this on the card. (For invitations *see page* 24.) Alternatively you can have a mulled wine party in winter and a "Pimms" party in summer.

Food at cocktail parties [1] is entirely a matter of taste and the hostess's imagination. Canapés, small hot sausages, biscuits with cheese dips, small sandwiches, or pieces of raw cauliflower with a mayonnaise dip are all excellent ideas. But many well known hostesses have learnt from experience not to offer too many varieties. The human animal is a creature of habit and tends to go for the old favourites—chipolatas, brown bread and smoked salmon sandwiches (you can cheat beautifully with best kipper, finely cut). Avoid food which makes a mess such as potato crisps or anything which crumbles or drips.

[1] See Nutshell Book No. 17, *Cocktail Fare* by Jean Balfour.

Most thoughtful guests leave before 8.30., and in fact they should, by the laws of etiquette, do so. Many younger hostesses have something cold in the fridge in case a few friends stay on.

Drinks Before Lunch on Sundays
This makes a delightful alternative to the cocktail party (particularly in the country) for busy people who work hard during the week in town. A dozen friends invited for 12 noon, when everyone is relaxed after a long lie-in or returning from church, is one of the most satisfactory ways of seeing friends regularly in a busy, crowded life. There is no need for "At Home" cards. A telephone call a week or so before the party is enough. Offer the same kind of drinks as you would at a cocktail party— but you do not need to pour them out beforehand—plus biscuits and a cheese dip. Clothes can be as informal as you like.

Buffets
Here is an excellent way of asking friends to a meal, particularly in summer when the food can all be cold and laid out attractively on a table, indoors or out. A buffet supper means you can entertain more friends than you would be able to at a sit-down dinner, yet it is more intimate than a cocktail party.

Do not invite too many guests and pack them in like sardines. Although guests help themselves, they must be able to sit down, even if it is only on cushions on the floor. All the cutlery should be laid out together on the table and the plates stacked. The host pours out the wine and hands round the glasses. At small wedding receptions or parties, a christening or silver wedding celebrations, a buffet can be fairly formal. It caters for more guests than

you could manage at a dinner party, yet is more cere-
monious than a cocktail party.

Buffets are excellent for wine and cheese parties for
older teenagers or for barbecues in the garden. Large
teas given by organisations such as The Women's Institute
or for members of groups such as musical societies, can also
be served in this way. At a buffet, it is easier to offer
cider, beer and soft drinks instead of wine. (It is impossible
to dispense with wine at a dinner party.)

Luncheons

A luncheon is one of the most formal ways in which women
can entertain one another. At a very smart lunch in town
it is wise to wear a hat, unless your hair has just emerged
from the hairdressers and you are groomed to perfection.
Suits or wool dresses are correct. Invitations for a very
formal luncheon are sent out on "At Home" cards a
fortnight or so prior to the event. If held for guests to
meet an important person, you write "To meet Mrs.
So-and-so" underneath the "Luncheon, 12.45 p.m."
written on the bottom right-hand corner of the card. Such
luncheons are an excellent way for organisers of charities
to get together to discuss a forthcoming arrangement.
On the card the hostess should write, for example, "To
discuss the Apple Ball, to be given in aid of the R.S.P.C.A."

If many people are invited, a buffet luncheon would be
more sensible or, if you can afford it, you can hire small
tables and chairs from most caterers and place four
guests at each table.

The time for guests to arrive at a luncheon party is
12.45 or 1 p.m. and guests must be *very* punctual. They
should leave between 2.30 and 3 p.m.

A luncheon party is made up of three courses like a
dinner party, but you can serve curries or stew, and cheeses

which are not served at dinners. A very formal luncheon, however, should be treated like a dinner.

Teenage Parties

These can range from a buffet evening meal, with dancing, to barbecue parties in the garden. A wine and cheese party is ideal for older teenagers, otherwise cider or a very mild wine cup can be provided. It is extraordinary how attractive a soft fruit drink can be made to look if you dress it up like a Pimms, with floating fruit in the jug and lots of ice and mint leaves.

It is more fun if the teenagers issue their own invitations on "At Home" cards. As such parties take place at home it is courteous for the teenagers to ask their parents to be there when the guests arrive and to introduce everyone to them. Then any sensible parent will melt away. The time should be stated on the card, "9 to 11 p.m." and other parents will bless you if you pop in towards the end of the party to see that arrangements are made for everyone to get home safely.

It is important, however, for parents to behave as guests, not as if they were running the whole thing, just as it is important for their children to treat them with courtesy and introduce them to their friends. Learning to vanish while still being around is a trick well worth cultivating in a house where adolescents and adults share a common life.

Coffee Parties

The coffee party enables women stuck at home to keep up contacts with neighbours and with friends who do not live too far away. Such a party is also a good way to meet and introduce a new arrival in the district to a group of others who live near her. A note can be sent to the new arrival asking her to come to coffee at 11 a.m. to meet some of her neighbours. Never ask too many at a time. Half a dozen is quite enough. Hot coffee, biscuits or pastries are all you need to provide. Friends can be asked by telephone, as it is a very informal way of entertaining and long notice need not be given. Guests should not stay more than an hour or an hour and a half.

Private Dances

A dance can be given at home, if there is a room large enough, or a marquee can be hired through a catering firm and put up in the garden, or a public hall, or a room in a hotel can be hired for the occasion. Most good caterers will put forward names of bands and can provide everything from extra glasses to chairs, tables and waiters.

"At Home" cards are sent out a month or so before the dance. If the event is a twenty-first birthday, this is stated on the card.

The parents and the child for whom the dance is being given stand just inside the door of the room where guests are being received and greet them *all*. It is wise to hire some kind of help to open the front door and see that guests leave their coats and wraps in the right room. If there is a large number of guests, then do see that tickets are given for each garment as if in a hotel. Invitations are usually sent out for 9 or 10 p.m. and you may provide a running buffet, wine and soft drinks. People rarely give sit-down dinners before a dance, and friends coming in a party will usually dine together beforehand.

Every single male guest should dance at least once with the girl for whom the dance is being given and with his hostess, or at least he should make the gesture (as most mothers will be too tired and pre-occupied to dance with everyone).

Subscription Dances

These are usually hunt balls held in a private country house, a hotel or a public hall, or any dance given in aid of a charity. Tickets can be obtained from patronesses or the Secretary. Sometimes the occasion is announced in newspapers or the patroness will ask her friends to get parties together. Each hostess will probably give dinner to her party before setting out to the dance. But a hostess should make it quite clear, if she asks friends to join her party, whether she is paying for their tickets or merely asking them to join her party and pay for their own tickets. Most people pay for their own tickets these days because the expenses can become phenomenal if a single person has to pay for six or eight tickets, although parents may often pay for the ticket of a young man who is accompanying their daughter. Guests buy their own drinks from the bar at these dances or, according to their pockets and generosity, rounds of drinks for their party who will probably be sitting together at a table.

It is permissible to dance with friends who are not in your party, although to disappear for the whole evening with someone else is very discourteous. Your first duty is to your hostess and to your party.

Twenty-first Birthday Parties

It is an important date in any person's life when they officially come of age. Friends and relations of all ages can be mixed at the gathering. It is an occasion for a marathon cocktail party, a buffet supper and dancing, or a dance. "At Home" cards are sent out four weeks or so beforehand. All guests should send or bring a present, and a toast is proposed by a great friend or a relation and drunk in champagne or wine.

Silver or Golden Wedding Parties

These are dates which mark twenty-five or fifty years of marriage. A birthday cake is *de rigueur*, and the party can either be a luncheon or dinner for relations and close friends, or a cocktail party. Most guests will bring a small present or send flowers.

Bridge Parties

Usually these are given from 3 to 6.30 p.m. and up to sixteen people are invited. Small tables are set out, each with four markers, pencils and two packs of cards. Women usually wear hats for these parties, but today it is not necessary, although you should never arrive in a sweater and skirt. An afternoon dress or suit is correct. Tea is served at a buffet around 4.30, and afterwards guests resume play.

Stakes should be low, so that winning or losing is never an embarrassment or a disaster. All card debts should be paid on the afternoon itself. A bridge party is often a way to raise money for some local charity. It can be given in a private house and guests will have bought tickets in advance, the price including tea or sherry afterwards.

Entertaining Wealthy Guests

Having guests far richer than you is often an embarrassment, but it should not be. Friendship is partly a matter of similar backgrounds but in terms of humanity it need not be that alone. Forget the marvellous house, food, etc. that they may have. Give them the best you can without making it ostentatious or incurring expense you cannot afford.

A good meal is a good meal, wherever it is, so offer your most successful dish and a good wine. Stifle the memory of champagne cocktails and get a bottle of really good Spanish sherry or offer an aperitif before the meal.

Behave with all the affection and respect you have for your guests as people, but do not get into a flap. It will make the evening a misery for you and an embarrassment for them.

Do not ask friends far richer than you to the kind of party which is completely unfamiliar to you. If you never have cocktail parties or black-tie dinners, ask them to Sunday lunch or a quiet but well-cooked dinner for four. Remember that the most attractive thing in the world is to be *liked*. Rich or poor, everyone needs that. Show them all your warmth and hospitality.

Bachelor Entertaining

This can be a headache both for men and women, yet single people often wish to return hospitality if they have a home of their own. Single men or women who have a flat of their own can always throw a small drink party, asking a particular friend to come early and help with drinks and handing round food. The secret is not to have too many guests. The Sunday morning drink party is an excellent way for unmarried people of both sexes to return hospitality.

It is difficult for a single woman to entertain friends in a restaurant unless she is very mature and sure of herself, but a man can return hospitality by giving a small luncheon or dinner party in a restaurant. If he is worried about the cost plus the embarrassment of six people searching through menus, he can order a set meal beforehand and know exactly how much the dinner will cost apart from drinks or wine; for the amount drunk can never be accurately assessed in advance. He can tell his guests that this restaurant is famous for such and such a dish and he has ordered a meal to complement it. His guests will be grateful, as it spares them wondering what he can afford on the menu.

A single woman can entertain three guests to supper in her flat (two of them men), and take them on to a theatre at no great cost and without the embarrassment of having to open her handbag to pay all the time. She will probably try to buy programmes, but if there are men in her party it is courteous if they get this small item and perhaps offer drinks during the interval.

If a woman has to take a man out to a restaurant on business and she is embarrassed about paying the bill, she can have a word with the headwaiter before her guest arrives and arrange to pay it on her way to the ladies' cloakroom before she leaves. This is only a suggestion to help the extra sensitive, because a business luncheon should not be embarrassing to either men or women.

Guests for the Week-end

In a world where we see our friends far too little and then mostly at a meal, it is one of the great pleasures of life to have them to stay for a day or two. Even in small houses or flats, and without a living-in help, such a stay can be organised so that both hosts and guests are completely at ease and enjoy it without getting too much in one another's way.

The hostess invites her guest or guests by letter three weeks or a fortnight before. She should say if she is having a dinner or cocktail party so that her guest knows what clothes to bring. She should state explicitly the duration of her invitation. "There is a good train from London which arrives here at 7.30 on Friday night and John will meet you at the station." or "Would you come and stay with us from Friday to Sunday?" or "Come in time for Saturday luncheon." A week-end ends on Sunday night, unless the hostess particularly asks you to stay until Monday morning.

When a guest arrives, take him up to his room so that he can wash and put away his things. In the bedroom there should be:

a) A hand towel and bath towel, folded, on a chair.
b) Flowers on the dressing table.
c) Some kind of fire if it is cold.
d) A new cake of soap if there is a wash-basin; otherwise new soap in the bathroom.
e) A hot water bottle.
f) A tin of biscuits beside the bed.
g) A couple of books and some magazines beside the bed.
h) A clock.
i) A box of matches.
j) Empty drawers with clean paper in them and at least four or five coat hangers in an empty part of the cupboard, even if you have clothes hanging in the rest of it.

Tell your guest that you will be having drinks in the drawing room at 6.30 p.m., so that he has fifteen minutes or half an hour in which to get ready, and knows when he should come down.

After dinner, it is entirely up to you to decide when to go to bed. On Friday night this should not be too late as most people are tired. Ask your guest if he likes a cup of tea in the morning.

Nowadays many hostesses offer to bring guests breakfast in bed as this solves several problems, e.g. what time to get up, and how to find time to clean and organise the household without having a guest under one's feet.

A guest should make his bed unless there is more

than one servant in the house, or the hostess tells him that it will be done for him.

You may have organised some activity for the morning and could say "Would you like to go fishing with John?" or "I'm going shopping at eleven o'clock. I'd love it if you would come with me." On the whole, however, a guest should be left to read the papers in the sitting-room, or to go for a walk if there is nothing going on other than household chores. A guest may safely come downstairs about ten o'clock with his breakfast tray, which he will put in the kitchen. A woman guest will wash up her dishes if there is no help in the house, but a man can leave them to be washed by his hostess.

Should breakfast be served in the dining-room, you must indicate at what time it will be put on the table and the guests will come down within fifteen minutes or so after that time. Each will help himself to whatever is laid on the table or the sideboard and have his breakfast quietly with a newspaper. There is no "must" about coming down to breakfast. It is the most informal "take-it-or-leave-it" meal of the day.

Always tell a guest at what time he can have a bath. Dressing bells have long been out of date, but at least an hour should be allowed for a guest to wash and change before dinner, leaving the host and hostess a little privacy to talk and tidy up, prepare meals and make plans.

A guest can offer to help wash up or lay the table but should not hang about all day saying "Can I help?" Some hostesses honestly prefer to wash up themselves, especially if the kitchen is small. A guest should then go off and read a book and leave her alone. It is up to a guest to gauge how much the hostess wants to be helped or wants him out of the way.

All week-end guests should bring a small gift for the

hostess—flowers, eggs, fruit or honey from the country; a bottle of wine, a special cheese, sweets or candied fruit from the town. A recently published book is an excellent gift and so are bath salts, three luxury soaps in a pretty box or a bottle of toilet water.

Thank-you letters must be written the day after a guest leaves.

Servants During a Week-end. If there is help in the house, the bed of each guest should be turned down at night and the dressing-gown and nightclothes laid out on it. A servant no longer unpacks a guest's entire suitcase, and indeed many guests would be embarrassed and even annoyed to find their perhaps untidy packing had been seen, and less than perfect toilet articles unpacked and put away.

Before leaving, the husband or the single guest should tip the servant or servants—but never the nanny. (For tips *see page* 110. For week-end clothes *see page* 114.)

10

ENTERTAINING OUTSIDE THE HOME

Today, many people have to entertain business acquaintances in restaurants or at the theatre, or have enough money to spare their wives the chores from time to time. Houses and flats are small, and sometimes people may find it more convenient to give a large cocktail party or dance in a hotel or at their club.

Restaurants
When you invite guests to dine in a restaurant, you should book a table and arrange to meet them in the foyer or in the cocktail lounge at least fifteen minutes before the time of the booking. You offer drinks, drink them in the lounge or bar, and then take your guests into the restaurant, having thought out the seating beforehand. So many people fumble about before going into restaurants, obviously wishing to let ladies go first, but it is much better if the host excuses himself and leads the way. He probably knows the table he has booked; if not, he can give his name to the head waiter, who will lead the party to the appropriate table.

You will seat your guests as at a private dinner party—most important woman on your right, etc. You can have chosen the menu previously to save time, or you can suggest various dishes so that guests know the kind of thing you can afford. It is always wise to give a lead. No guest should ever decide upon very expensive items like smoked salmon, caviar or oysters, unless the host has first suggested them.

Guests should indicate their choice to the host, who gives the order to the waiter and calls for the wine waiter. It is not necessary for the host to ask his guests which wine they prefer. He is supposed to have enough expertise to be able to choose the right wine to go with the food selected, although he should ask if anyone would like a soft drink. After dinner, liqueurs or brandy may be offered at the table. This is not so necessary at luncheon, although at a man's business lunch these are usually offered.

Should there be dancing in the restaurant, the most important man should ask his hostess to dance. Every man in the party should dance with the hostess and at least once with the other women guests. No woman should ever be left alone at the table.

It is more courteous and less embarrassing if the host pays the bill away from the table.

Guests should start to leave around 11 to 11.30 p.m. The host should offer to give lifts, and should certainly see a single woman home or see that another guest takes her home.

The same procedure is followed at the theatre. You may like to ask your guests to come to your home for a drink beforehand. You will either take all your guests in your car or in a taxi, or arrange that another guest with a car takes some of the party. You will seat your guests as carefully in the theatre as at a dinner party, pay for programmes and take the least desirable seat yourself. You should also offer drinks during the interval, but it is quite correct for a guest to offer to pay for a second round. You should always indicate to your guests how you wish them to dress.

Guests do not speak to a waiter themselves, but indicate all their desires to the host, who passes them on. Guests do not complain to a waiter if something is wrong with the food or spilt upon the table. They tell the host. Guests do not offer to pay for *anything* except that second round of drinks at the theatre, a taxi or their personal tips in the cloakroom.

Men will leave coats in the cloakroom, but a woman usually takes hers into the restaurant with her and drapes it over the back of her chair.

Night-Clubs

With some clubs you may have to be proposed as a member by a friend, but there are clubs where you can become a nominal member for the evening. You book your table for around 10 p.m. and you may eat a dinner or merely have drinks and sandwiches.

Nowadays there are few night-clubs (if any) where dinner jackets are *de rigueur*. A dark city suit with a white shirt and collar, is always correct, and women should wear cocktail dresses. They should also wear a fur coat, wrap, stole or evening coat. Day-time tweeds worn with silk dresses look simply ghastly.

Bills at night-clubs should be paid in cash, as cheques are not always acceptable. Always take enough money with you.

If two couples want to go out "Dutch," it is much better if one man pays and the other arranges to pay him later. Two people scrabbling about to work out the exact change are undignified and cause embarrassment to others.

Basic Table Manners

Men always wait for women to be seated first, and assist

95

them in this. Table napkins are unfolded and placed upo
the knees. They are never tucked into clothes and ar
never used to scrub the mouth or to wipe up a mess on th
table. You wipe your mouth and fingers gently, and alway
leave a table napkin crumpled beside your place when yo
leave the table. Never fold a napkin up. Napkin ring
are never used for parties or at meals with guests.

Soup is drunk from a soup spoon, from the sid
nearest you.

Hors d'oeuvres are eaten with a fork only, unless ther
are large chunks of sausage which have to be cut.

Melon is eaten with a spoon.

Bread is never cut, but broken with the fingers and eate
piece by piece.

Puddings are always eaten with a fork or a fork an
spoon, never with a spoon alone, unless they are cream
or mousses which are served with a small spoon.

Oysters are eaten with a small fork. There is no ru
of etiquette which demands that you should swallo
an oyster whole. You would loose its entire savou
You do not, of course, masticate it like chewing-gum.

Peas are eaten with a knife and fork, never with th
fork turned up.

Asparagus is eaten with the fingers, dipped in butter c
sauce and carried to the mouth. Finger bowls are alway
used when eating asparagus. Asparagus served as a veg
etable is eaten with a knife and fork.

Bones should never be picked up in your fingers, excep
in the privacy of the family.

Pâté or *caviar* is served with butter, toast and lemo
You break the toast and butter it before you add som
pâté or caviar, and eat it with your fingers bit by bi
Never spead a large piece of toast and bite bits off. (Thi
also applies to eating cheese.)

Dessert or Fresh Fruit is eaten with a small silver knife and fork which are presented to each guest on the fruit plate. Apples and pears are cut into quarters and the core removed, then eaten with both knife and fork. Oranges and bananas are seldom offered at dessert. Raspberries and strawberries are eaten with a spoon and fork, but grapes, cherries and lichees are eaten with the fingers. Pips are returned from the mouth to the plate in the palm of the hand. Finger bowls are always used after eating fruit.

If you find a fruit stone in your mouth while eating a compote, remove it on the spoon, but do not actually spit it on to the spoon. Pieces of unexpected bone or gristle should be quietly removed with the fingers, and placed on the plate within the curve of your hand.

A Knife is always held with the tip of the handle in the palm of the hand—never between first finger and thumb like a pencil.

Do not throw back your head and drink large gulps of wine. Sip it gently.

In Britain, *hands* are always kept on the lap when you are not eating, although on the Continent hands are placed on the table beside the plate.

Never drink with your mouth full.

If you do not like something which is offered to you, take a very small portion and try to eat it. Refuse second helpings or vegetables by all means, but it is discourteous to refuse any of the courses.

Never cut up all your food before you eat it. Cut each mouthful, and do not mash up fruit or vegetables.

Each guest should take care to talk to guests both on his right and on his left.

No guest should ever smoke at table unless his hosts offer cigarettes.

No guest should ever leave the table until the hostess gets up.

If a servant is waiting at table, food is handed to you on your left. You help yourself without looking at the servant and you do not thank him. You can murmur "No thank you" if you are offered a second helping or do not wish to drink wine.

11

CHILDREN

There is no doubt that in countries, such as France, where a definite code of etiquette is impressed upon and observed by children from a fairly early age, they are at their most charming and at their least obnoxious on public occasions. The person who benefits almost more than anyone else is the child himself who, in a confusing world, at least knows a few simple rules for what must be the most difficult period in a lifetime of social intercourse.

The gap between the generations is difficult enough to bridge, but for a small child it can be an agony and a bewilderment. It is a great help if he knows *exactly* how to behave and is not left to flounder in front of an array of enormous human beings who gawp at him, ply him with silly questions and bestow on him compliments of doubtful value.

A definite but simple code of behaviour for social occasions saves a child from the terrifying uncertainty so common with the very young when faced with an unknown and grown-up world (and even when faced with those of his own generation whom he does not already know), particularly when shyness is an agony and the child is perhaps not naturally forthcoming. It is far easier for a child to learn good habits first, rather than start with bad ones because his parents think he is too young to understand explanations, and then have to be weaned from them when he begins to be set in his ways through spoiling or simply having been left to his own devices. (People become set in their ways far younger than is popularly supposed!) Teach gently, explain afterwards.

First of all, a child should be introduced to another person, whether grown up or not, as if he were a perfectly normal human being. "This is John, my son," or "This is John," *never* "This is my little boy" or "This is our dear little boy." Children from a very early age hate being made to feel foolish, and so long as things are made perfectly understandable to their less developed mentalities they should be treated like any normal person.

It is also extremely rude and humiliating if the parents tell friends how awful the child is or make any disparaging remark in front of him because they think the child will not understand. This is one of the most serious and damaging ways of behaving badly—it has lasting effects and may result in a lifelong inferiority complex. Those who suffered from this kind of thing when children should never, never inflict it upon their own children. Tick them off soundly in the privacy of the family but never make them feel humiliated in public.

A child should be taught to hold out his hand and say "How do you do?" when introduced to, or greeted by, someone, not to smirk or make any other remarks. He should learn that any personal remarks such as "I don't like you!" or "What a funny lady!" or anything of that nature is rude and hurtful, and any such feelings should be kept strictly for family discussion.

Although children must always feel free to ask questions and not be afraid of talking when in the company of their elders, they should be told that to interrupt at meals, particularly when guests are present, is the height of rudeness. It does no one any harm to listen, particularly when very young, for here lies a great opportunity to learn something useful about the art of conversation, and it is extraordinary how much can sink into the youngest mind. (This is assuming that there *is* some conversation and not a series of grunts and questions about domestic matters alone!) Furthermore, this is the one time in life when one can enjoy listening without having to think up a fascinating reply, a pleasure which must soon depart in a world of competitive expression. This can be explained to a child quite simply and literally.

As soon as he can write, a child should be told of the importance of thank-you letters, rapidly written and dispatched after receiving presents, even if it is a little tedious and there are other and more exciting things to be done. This is the kind of habit which makes for pleasant teenagers and delightful grown-ups. Sometimes people grow up never to thank or appreciate properly, through no real fault of their own. They have never been taught that this is one of the basic courtesies and one of the best small pleasures one person can give to another.

Apart from teaching such minor facts as that it is unattractive to shout, show off, throw things about or make stupid faces, grab, dive for the largest cake or take a second helping which leaves nothing for the next person, remember to encourage those habits which, if impressed upon the young more often, might eventually fill the world with far more charming people than already inhabit it! Charles Kingsley's "Mrs. Do-as-you-would-be-done-by" would be an excellent example to quote and Sir Philip Sidney's "Thy necessity is yet greater than mine" is perhaps the most profound courtesy ever offered to a fellow man.

The art of good manners, or the rules of etiquette, whichever you prefer to call it, is something which should not be taught in a series of "don'ts" but as a constructive code of behaviour. Not "People will dislike you if . . .", but "You will be a much more pleasant person if . . .", and "As a mark of pride in yourself as a lady, or a gentleman, you should. . . ." It is teaching children to value other human beings, to treat them with consideration and to recognise in them the same dignity and importance as everyone, let us admit it, sees in himself.

But it is also important for parents not to be rude to their children. This is a part of etiquette which is often neglected. Children have every right to be treated with courtesy, and no child is going to grow up with a sense of good manners if he is constantly treated rudely by his elders. This kind of thing can rankle and make the child swear to himself that when he grows up he will have his own back on society. I am sure it is such children who grow up into the aggressive and ill-mannered boors who appear too frequently upon the social scene.

Children's Parties

For children up to the age of about ten, parties are held between 3 and 6 p.m. Between the age of ten and becoming a teenager, many children are bored to tears by the conventional party and tend to reject an entertainment they consider babyish. Parents can then sigh with relief until the children are old enough to want to organise parties themselves. Of course, this varies from child to child and family to family.

It is wise to have children within a fairly close age group to avoid trouble, as children are terrible "age snobs." A party should be planned like a military campaign, including games, food and perhaps an entertainment such as a conjurer, clown or film.

Tea is a sit-down affair with a festive table laid out with

the conventional food all children love—ice cream, sandwiches, cakes, small hot sausages, jelly, lemonade, orangeade and milk. The entertainment, if there is one, should take place after tea when the children begin to get restive.

If nannies come with the children, they usually stay and are given tea in another room. If parents bring their children, they usually retire home thankfully until the time to pick them up, unless the children are very small indeed.

There is a convention, right or wrong, that every child should bring a small present to the host. These need not cost more than a couple of shillings, but should be prettily wrapped up. A small toy, a notebook and bright red pencil, a piece of furniture for a doll's house, or a story book, are all excellent presents.

One of the problems is what on earth to do with mothers who turn up a little early to fetch their offspring. Should one or should one not offer them a drink? The bright hostess will have a tray with glasses and a decanter of sherry at one end of the room or in another room. Each mother will be welcomed and asked if she would like a glass of sherry. This will keep her occupied while her child is told to go and put his or her coat on. A trail of restless mothers hanging about at the end of a party can spell disaster.

12

THE GIVING OF PRESENTS

The giving of presents outside the family circle and close friends can be a tricky business. Too often the whole thing misfires, which is a pity, because presents are a sign of affection, gratitude, thoughtfulness and a desire to please.

Two Rules:
1. Never give a present which might be thought to be a bribe.
2. Never return with another present soon after you have been given one.

The Hostess Present

Never arrive at any kind of formal dinner party *with* a bunch of flowers. Send them before or after. Nothing is more harassing to a busy hostess than to have to take flowers into the kitchen, put them in a vase and return them to the drawing room when she should be attending to her guests. A bunch of flowers on any other occasion is a delightful gesture and is entirely up to your generosity.

The Week-end Guest should always bring a small present for his hostess. *See page* 91-2.

Presents to Hospital Nurses

Some matrons disapprove unconditionally. The International Code, observed in fourteen countries, says that nurses are not supposed to receive anything apart from their salaries. Many of us, however, feel grateful if a nurse has been particularly helpful and kind. One way of saying "thank you" without causing embarrassment is to present the sister with a large box of sweets for all the nurses on the ward or flowers for the office. A couple of theatre tickets sent to a nurse at the nurses' home is a nice gesture and will not embarrass her among the other nurses. What anyone chooses to give in the privacy of his home, afterwards, is entirely his own business.

Presents to Invalids

Anyone who has been very ill will know that sweets, chocolates and cakes are not always the panacea for depression that they are often thought to be. They can turn the stomach of a delicate patient. But toilet water, talcum powder, a super soap, a bedjacket are very welcome and thoughtful presents. For men (and women too) a good book, magazines, writing paper and (if it is allowed) a quarter bottle of champagne or a bottle of wine are excellent morale boosters.

Office Presents

Communal presents to those who are leaving or getting married are merely a matter of collecting money from the rest of the staff in a department.

There are often arguments about presents at Christmas time. Some offices forbid them altogether upon the premises. One of the nicest ways of dealing with Christmas presents is for every member of the staff to buy something small which does not cost more than 2s. 6d. or 5s. These are then wrapped up and put in a tombola at the Christmas party. Everyone draws a present and everyone has paid for one. This is fun and eliminates the problems of jealousy or overspending.

A present to the boss is appropriate only on special

occasions such as a business anniversary, a retirement or marriage. A collection is made, the present purchased by senior members of the staff and the presentation made either at the usual tea break in one of the offices or over drinks at a party, if one is to be given. A senior staff member makes the presentation, with perhaps a small speech of congratulation.

Wedding Presents can be anything, according to your pocket and your friendship with the bride or groom. Such presents are usually fairly substantial compared with most other presents, and should preferably be things useful for a future home. Some brides have lists at a large store near their homes. It is always wise to ask if there is one, as this eliminates your sending something the couple may have already. The list should contain items of all prices and when one is bought it is crossed off. A wedding is one of the few occasions when money can be given, usually as a cheque. Presents are sent after the invitations have been received, usually to the bride's home. You address the card to both the bride and bridegroom.

Your Husband's Secretary

Should your husband wish to give his secretary a present (and you know her), it is more courteous and proper that the present should come from both of you. If you do not know her at all, your husband should mention that you chose the present and that it is from both of you for all she has done in the past year.

If both husband and wife sign the card inside, the secretary should thank her boss in person and write a note to his wife.

Giving Money

Money is usually given only to close members of a family (children, nephews, nieces, godchildren). Money should not be given to people older than yourself as a rule (but there are always exceptions). Money can always be given for a wedding present.

Money is also given as Christmas boxes to postmen, milkmen, dustmen and your daily help. Always give it in an envelope, never from hand to hand. Try to give it in person so that you can be thanked on the spot, for this avoids embarrassing anyone who does not know how to thank in any other way.

Presents Between Single Men and Women

Not so long ago there was a rigid code about this. No man gave jewellery, personal things or very valuable presents and women never gave men presents unless they were engaged. Today this has changed to a certain extent, but the principle is still right.

A man can always send a girl flowers, fruit or sweets. A girl who knows a man well and wants to give him a present can give a book or a record, particularly at Christmas time or if she wants to make a gesture of thanks for being taken out and entertained over a period of time. She may also buy a couple of theatre tickets for a special play or a show if she does not like the feeling of being paid for all the time.

13

TIPPING

This often causes far more worry than it need. There are three facts to be borne in mind. The first is that tipping is not an obligation in any but a purely moral sense. It is the giving of a gratuity or "kindness" to anyone who gives personal service. Secondly, there are, rightly or wrongly, certain jobs whose salaries are established on the assumption that they will be made up by tips. Whether this is right remains a fair subject for argument, but there it is.

Thirdly, you are under no obligation to tip if you feel you have been badly served, but you should say so, quietly and courteously.

In most *hotels* and *restaurants* tipping is based on 15% to 20% of the bill. You must look to see if this sum has been added to the bill. This applies particularly on the Continent. In France, you always tip the wine waiter.

You do not tip the *owner* of a restaurant or business, or any *airline* employee.

In a *hotel*, you tip the chambermaid about 10% of the room bill and the waiter in the dining room about 10% of the bill for meals. If you have been staying for a holiday, it is usual to give the *head waiter* a good tip if he has helped by getting a special table, hurrying up the service or any other small favours. The *hall porter* usually gets a tip if he has called taxis, looked up theatres or provided information and personal service. *Liftmen* and other servants who carry luggage to and from rooms are tipped on the spot.

You always tip a servant in a *rooming house*, but not the proprietor. (If he has any sense he will add a percentage to your bill for service when only he or members of his family wait on you.)

At the *hairdressers*, for a shampoo, cut and set you tip about 1s. 6d. to 2s., and to the apprentice who washes your hair you give 6d. to 1s.

You tip in bars only if the drinks have actually been brought to your table. The same applies in coffee bars.

Cloakrooms. You should look at the saucer where the attendant usually leaves the kind of coin she expects, and tip accordingly. Thus in a very smart hotel, you will see two shilling pieces and half-crowns, while in a store there will be sixpences and threepenny bits.

Taxi drivers should be tipped 6d. for fares up to 4s., about 9d. to 1s. 6d. for fares up to 10s., and so on. These sums are purely arbitrary. There is no hard and fast rule. Taxi drivers who drive you late at night expect larger tips.

There is no need to tip a *doorman* outside a shop, restaurant or hotel unless you ask him to fetch a taxi or he holds an umbrella over you in the rain while you wait. Give him 6d. unless the hotel is very grand, then 1s. or 2s. according to his services. Merely opening a car door is no reason for getting a tip.

Many people wonder if they should tip the *pump attendant* at a filling station. This is not at all necessary unless he has performed some service such as wiping your windscreen, testing tyres, etc. Some people who use the same garage regularly and get good service like to tip their particular attendant once in a while as a mark of appreciation.

Any *waitress* service should be tipped, even for a cup of tea. Leave 3d. or 6d. beside your plate.

On train journeys, you tip the *porter* who carries your bag—1s. or so for a single bag and 2s. for three. *Sleeping berth attendants* who bring you tea or perform any personal service receive about 2s. 6d.

You tip *removal men* who have carried furniture at least £1 for a day's work, this sum to be shared between them.

On board ship (on a voyage longer than one or two days) you tip the *cabin steward* about 30s., *bath steward* about 10s. and the *deck steward* (if you sit out on deck regularly and he gets you a chair) about 10s. Your *waiter* at table will get around 30s., and about the same to the *head waiter* if he has performed any particular services. You obviously tip more after a very long passage or a cruise. Tips should be about 20% of the price of your ticket.

If you stay in a *private house* where there is one *woman servant*, you will tip her 5s. to 10s. for a week-end. If there is a *man servant* or *butler* your husband will tip the manservant around 15s. and the butler £1.

Men invited to *shoot* for a week-end or long week-end should tip a *head gamekeeper* about £1, and £2 to the loader. But it is perfectly correct to ask the host or one of the fellow guests what the form is, as these tips vary in various houses and parts of the country.

Grooms are tipped up to 2s. if a horse is hired from a riding stable, and members of a *Hunt* should tip hunt servants at Christmas.

Never tip *club servants.*

14

CLOTHES AND APPEARANCE

How you look can be an indication of your character, social status, breeding and consideration for the feelings of others, quite apart from the desire to make yourself look as attractive as possible.

Personal taste governs the choice of dress but there are certain kinds of clothes for different occasions which, although styles may vary from generation to generation, are considered to be right according to the unwritten laws of etiquette.

Appearance, as an outward indication of the kind of person you are, can make or mar a first impression at an interview or an occasion when you are meeting people you wish to think well of you. This has nothing to do with being in the *avant-garde* of fashion. It has a lot to do with looking clean, well groomed and omitting any flashy or vulgar accessories or mixtures of colour.

Basic Principles

Good grooming is essential even if you cannot afford a great many clothes. Hair should be clean, tidy and well arranged. Hands and nails should always be clean and look cared for, stockings unwrinkled.

Hats

Hats should always be worn by women at weddings, funerals, christenings and any church service, also at important official luncheons, most race meetings (small hats) and Royal Ascot where you can wear cartwheels, or anything which is beautiful and smart, on top of your dress or coat. Men will wear grey toppers and morning dress. Formal hats for women and grey toppers are also worn at royal garden-parties.

Younger women who have just had their hair done can go hatless to luncheon in a restaurant or to an interview. Cocktail party veiling hats are not essential but look pretty at very grand parties, especially on an older woman.

Never wear a very large hat at huge gatherings (such as royal garden-parties or official cocktails), or in any confined space. They tend to look like a sea of dinner plates and can easily be knocked off. Small hats also look much better at smart luncheons.

Nowadays there are few occasions when men *have* to wear a hat. They wear grey toppers with morning dress at weddings or Royal Ascot. They really should wear a black hat at a funeral. Doffing the hat is a mark of respect —and one must have something to doff!

Jewellery

It used to be said that diamonds should not be worn during the day-time, but the woman who is lucky enough to possess a diamond brooch can wear it on the lapel of her coat or suit at a very smart luncheon. Jewellery during the day-time should be kept to an absolute minimum. Dangling ear-rings, or more than one piece of jewellery, should not be worn during the day.

There are such beautiful costume jewels today that, very sensibly, the laws of etiquette have relaxed as far as they are concerned, but keep imitation diamonds and anything that sparkles for the evening. Plain gilt or good imitation pearls are perfectly correct for the day.

Tiaras can be worn by married women at dances or

functions where royalty is present, or really grand occasions such as a hunt ball.

Women should wear rings only on their engagement fingers. A signet ring should bear one's family coat of arms but never initials. Men wear them on the little finger of the left hand, as do women, but only if they wear no other rings.

If a man really wants to look dignified and conservative he should avoid tie clips, expanding gold straps for his watch, and anything but the most unobtrusive studs, waistcoat buttons and links. Tie pins have come back lately for all clothes but sportswear. But they should be discreet—a plain gold knot for the day and a single pearl in the evening.

Gloves

Women should always wear gloves when they are meeting others, at an interview or to enter a smart restaurant. Always take your gloves off at a cocktail party to eat canapés and drink your cocktail. Forget the old custom of taking off your right-hand glove and draping it from your left hand while you drink. Take both your gloves off and put them in your handbag if you are eating, drinking, shaking hands *and* carrying a handbag. On the whole, women shake hands, upon entering a room, with their gloves on. Men must always take them off.

If long gloves are worn at an official dinner, take them off before eating. The old custom of unbuttoning the hand part and pushing it back over the arm is extremely ugly and uncomfortable.

When a woman goes for an interview, she shakes hands with her gloves on, then takes one or both off and places them in her lap while she is talking. She puts on her gloves again at the end of the interview.

Gloves need not necessarily be of suède or leather, but they should be very clean and if possible not in bright colours. White, black and all colours of beige or cream, down the gamut of browns, are the safest buys. No embroidery, beading, eyelets or sewn ruffling should ever appear on a good glove.

There is no occasion when men *must* wear gloves, but if they are going to have them, they must *wear* them, not carry them.

Clothes for A Country Visit

A hostess should always warn her guests if there is going to be a dinner party or a cocktail party at her house so that they know what clothes to bring. If there is a dance, she should state what kind of a dance it is—white tie and ball dress, or black tie and simpler long dresses or even short ones. Many dinner parties in the country are black-tie affairs, and the classic little black dress or a long-sleeved and fairly décolleté velvet dress are ideal for women in winter. A simple silk or smart cotton dress is sufficient in summer.

If you are unsure whether a dance is going to be very grand or merely a "hop", it is wise to have a long evening skirt, say in black taffeta. You can take along a silk shirt in a beautiful colour, a décolleté black sweater and a strapless top to match, and you will be all right for any occasion.

A jersey or knitted suit is excellent for country week-ends. It will pack without creasing, and you can wear the skirt in the morning with a chunky sweater, add its jacket at luncheon, and in the evening with a silk shirt and beads.

Although you can wear any kind of high-heeled shoe in the evening, you should bring a pair of classic shoes with lowish heels for the day and some walking shoes for humping round the village and for attending a meet or point-to-point, unless it is real gumboot weather.

You should have at least one skirt which has a deep pleat or pleats, so that you do not get stuck half-way when climbing over a style or jumping a ditch.

The most suitable coat to wear for walks, beagling, following hunts on foot or at point-to-points is a sheepskin jacket or, if it is less cold, a three-quarter camel or tweed coat. In summer, most cotton dresses and little jumper suits of artificial fibre mixtures will see you through the day.

You can wear lacy thick-knit stockings in the country or coloured thick stockings (scarlet with a red plaid skirt or dark green with a grey flannel or dark green plaid, but not black stockings).

A man should take one dark suit for the evenings unless the hostess asks him to bring a dinner jacket. He should have a tweed suit for the day or a tweed jacket and a pair of military cord trousers. (Sweaters and corduroys should be taken for "mucking about.")

Golf Clothes

In winter, a woman can wear a pleated tweed skirt or a skirt with a deep central pleat which does not hang too heavily and a short jacket in suède or a warm fabric and a very warm, thick sweater underneath. Her stockings should be thicker than usual and her shoes flat, laced up or buckled, not the kind of shoe that looks like a slipper. In summer she should wear a shirt with a skirt, or a shirt-waist dress in cotton or linen mixtures with enough fullness in the skirt to allow movement, but not too much.

Tennis Clothes

These should be in classical white for both men and women, but unless you are going to play in a tournament or with tennis fiends, you are safe with a coloured shirt and shorts. Women should never wear shorts so tiny that they look like bathing suits, but they can wear slightly longer shorts, abbreviated skirts or tennis dresses.

Men wear white shirts and long white trousers or knee-length shorts. Both men and women *must* wear white tennis shoes and socks.

Riding Clothes

Jodhpurs are the classic dress although if you hunt regularly you can wear breeches and jack-boots. Jodhpurs should be beige and sweaters beige, yellow or brown, hacking jackets brownish and boots brown. Women who hunt a great deal usually wear dark blue or black jackets, fawn breeches, jack-boots, white stocks, yellow vests and string gloves, but if you are an infrequent follower to hounds, and the hunt is not one of the very grand ones, you can ride to hounds in jodhpurs, hacking jackets, bowler or hunting cap. If you have any doubts, telephone the hunt secretary. Men should never wear pink coats unless they are members of the hunt.

The Hostess at a Dinner Party

The hostess should never be more formally dressed than her guests, so she should make quite clear to them the kind of clothes she wants them to wear. But it is her privilege to wear a long skirt, providing the top is not too décolleté, while guests are in short skirts. Guests do not arrive for a dinner party in long skirts unless they are going on to a dance.

Dress for Restaurants

Dark suits are *de rigueur* for men, although at many of the top hotels men may wear dinner jackets in the evening, especially when there is dancing. Women at luncheon can wear suits, a formal coat and dress underneath, and usually a hat. In the evening, women dress according to the men who are with them. If dinner jackets are being worn, they will wear very dressy cocktail dresses. If the men are in dark suits, either a simple cocktail dress, a black dress or even a dark and sophisticated day dress is adequate.

Dress for Night-clubs

Although many young girls and their escorts may end an evening at a night-club in the full splendour of ball dresses, white ties or dinner jackets, it is perfectly correct for men to wear dark suits and the women cocktail dresses, even very simple ones.

Dress for the Theatre and Opera

It really is a great pity that many people go to the theatre in tweed skirts and coats, duffel-coats and such like. The correct dress is dark suits for men and a simple cocktail dress with a fur wrap, fur coat or evening coat for women. At first nights people in the stalls and circles usually wear dinner jackets and cocktail dresses and sometimes long dresses.

Dress for the Informal Dinner Party

Women are always correctly dressed in a little black "something-or-other," a dark wool dress or a cocktail suit. Dark suits should be worn by the men.

Dress for the Formal Dinner Party

These may be "black-tie" affairs, in which case you will be warned by your hostess. This means cocktail dresses for women, as décolleté as they like but never strapless, and as much jewellery as they care to wear. If black ties are not mentioned, the men will wear dark suits.

Decorations for Men

If the word "Decorations" appears on an invitation card, it means that those who have any orders or medals will wear them on their full evening dress (white tie). Most men will have them made up into miniatures and pin them on. Miniatures (neck decorations and stars), are not usually worn with dinner jackets.

Public Dinners and Official Evening Receptions

You will be told on the card what is expected. "Evening Dress" means dinner jackets for the men, but it is not incorrect to turn up with a white tie. If the occasion is grand, long dresses are suitable for the women, but not full-skirted ball dresses. Short evening dresses are also correct. "Dress Optional" means dark suits for the men and cocktail dresses for the women.

At official evening receptions, men will wear dark suits and women cocktail dresses, sometimes with little evening hats or veiling head-dresses. Always telephone the secretary if you are in doubt.

Royal Ascot

Hats at their most exotic appear at Ascot. Women wear formal dresses and coats or very elegant summer suits. (Mink stoles and too many geegaws always look dreadful.) Men wear morning dress and grey toppers.

Henley

A pretty summer dress or a linen suit is ideal for Henley, unless you are invited to one of the enclosures; then you dress up a little more and wear a hat. Men wear light suits.

Summer Holiday at a Smart Seaside Resort

Apart from beach wear and swimsuits, a woman should take at least a couple of pretty sleeveless cotton dresses to wear in the evening, and a simple linen or cotton shift or shirt-waist or jumper suit to wear at restaurants in the town and for cocktails at a casino. On the Continent, women wear silk trousers and shirts in the evening at some resorts.

Every woman going to a Latin country should take at least one dress with sleeves or a cardigan and silk scarf to wear when visiting churches. Be careful about bikinis, and gauge what the others are wearing, as these are not always welcome in parts of Spain and Italy. A shift in a beautiful cotton print or towelling with buttons all the way down is one of the most useful garments for holidays anywhere. It can be worn over a swimsuit when returning to the hotel or walking through a town where you do not feel you can wear shorts. It is easy to slip on and off, even over a damp swimsuit, and you will cause no offence in countries where women are expected to be adequately covered up.

Clothes on Board Ship

For a long voyage, or on a cruise, it is wise for a man to take a dinner jacket and for a woman to have a couple of cocktail dresses and one long dress for dinner or gala evenings. Other clothes should be simple and comfortable. Women should take some flat-heeled shoes for walking the decks.

Ask your travel agent if you are in doubt. He will know the form for each liner.

Travelling

A knitted, unlined coat is excellent for plane or train because it is light, uncrushable and warm. Unless you are off on a quick hop by plane to Paris, it is unsuitable to wear a hat other than a jersey turban, beret or head-scarf. Shoes should be comfortable, and it is wise to wear gloves because hands get really filthy. A "sporting look" is the most elegant look for travelling. You should never look "towny."

Dressing for the Office

Wear what you would wear during the day if you were going out to coffee or seeing people. A wool dress, jumper suit, sweaters, blouses and skirts are all suitable (although these should never be sloppy or look as if they were just making for the ski slopes). Shoes should be plain high-heeled pumps. No open sandals or fancy stockings should ever appear at the office. You should always wear stockings, on even the hottest day.

During the summer, never wear a dress that is too décolleté or skimpy. Clients might easily judge your firm by the looks of its employees, at first glance. It is your duty to your employer to look clean, well groomed and suitably dressed. Men should wear dark suits and black shoes. No man should ever wear brown shoes with a dark city suit.

15

TAKING OUT A GIRL

As etiquette is made up of a number of unwritten rules of behaviour designed to make the running of life much smoother, it is wise to know them when taking out a girl as she might easily be offended and decide to stop seeing you long before she finds out about your beautiful soul!

Such are the conventions of society, that if a man wishes to ask a girl out he should expect to pay for the *entire* expenses of the evening, *at first*. If, later on when they get to know each other better, they decide to share expenses, it is entirely up to them.

This is becoming much more common today when girls earn substantial salaries, but it is up to the girl to suggest it tactfully, as there are still men who do not feel happy about letting a girl pay for herself.

If "going Dutch" is agreed upon for the evening, it is much more courteous and less embarrassing if the girl gives the man her share of the money beforehand or they decide to work it out afterwards. To scrabble about in her handbag or work out expenses *in situ* is embarrassing and degrading for the man. It is, alas, up to the girl to suggest this, unless you know her very well indeed.

The first time a man asks a girl out he should suggest something specific like dinner in a restaurant, a theatre, a cinema or an outing to do something in particular. The afternoon or evening should be planned like a campaign. Most girls prefer this approach to being asked "What would you like to do?", especially if they do not know how much a man can afford. As friendship progresses, plans can be discussed and decisions made in a far more democratic way.

Nothing is more depressing or irritating to a girl than to be constantly asked by a man she does not know well what she would like to do, where she wants to go and what she wants to do next. It is a matter of basic psychology that women (as a whole) like to be led in these matters and have things chosen for them, and they will sit happily through a play that bores them to distraction if they find a man attractive.

In the evening, a man should offer to fetch the girl from her home rather than make arrangements to meet her at a certain place, unless this proves to be absolutely impossible due to time and distance. If she lives with her parents she can introduce him briefly, but need not ask him to have a drink.

If a girl lives by herself and does not want the man to fetch her until she knows him better, she can say it is more convenient to meet him at the place of entertainment, and he should not insist. She does not have to give him a reason.

A man should let the girl know what kind of restaurant he is taking her to, so that she knows what to wear and is not embarrassed by arriving over or under-dressed. He can mention that everyone seems to dress up for that performance or that he is wearing a black tie to go out dancing.

A man should always open doors of cars and taxis and see the girl is comfortably seated before seating himself. If he has to park his car some way off from the restaurant or theatre, he should offer to drop her at the entrance so that she can wait for him in the foyer.

A man should get out of a taxi first and turn to help the girl out. She should then walk slowly into the entrance of the restaurant while he pays the fare and then joins her to go inside. She should not stand beside him, breathing down his neck, or rush in and go straight to the ladies' cloakroom leaving him to wonder where on earth she has gone.

A man leaves his coat in the cloakroom and a woman keeps hers on. She leaves only a mackintosh or heavy tweed coat in the ladies' cloakroom. Once seated, she will slip off her wrap or coat and the man will help her drape it over the back of her chair.

A man should never refer to the girl with him as "She" or "Her" to the waiter or attendant. He should say "The lady would like. . . ."

Choosing a meal need not worry a man if he has a careful budget to follow. He can say "Chicken is fabulous here," indicating the kind of dish which is within his means. The girl can choose a dish a couple of shillings more or less but not something far more expensive *or* the cheapest dish on the menu. Both would be embarrassing for her host. Pudding should be offered, but if the meal has been fairly expensive the girl would be thoughtful if she said she just wanted coffee and that was all.

At dinner, it is expected that a man offers wine (it need be only a glass, as most wines can be bought by the glass). He does not have to offer a drink beforehand unless he wants to, nor need he offer a liqueur afterwards. If the girl says she wants a soft drink, and the man wants something stronger, he should ask her if she minds. A man chooses wine without asking the girl which she would like.

A girl out with a man only tips the cloakroom attendant

if she has left something in the ladies' cloakroom or goes there to powder her nose.

While it is a delightful gesture for a man to bring or send flowers to a girl's home, *he does not bring a flower for her to wear* on her dress. This is partly due to fashion, because women no longer wear flowers, and partly because the custom has fallen into abeyance. A kind-hearted girl would be embarrassed if she felt she *had* to pin on a flower in order not to upset her escort.

It is entirely up to the girl to say when she wants to go home. A man should always take her home, unless she lives so far away that she has a train to catch. Then, he should take her to the station and see her off. But it is wrong as well as discourteous to let young girls go home alone late at night.

If a man has to get up early in the morning and the night appears to be dragging on, he can tell the girl that they must leave at a certain time and explain why. It is always better to explain *why* than to watch the clock nervously and rush the whole thing.

It is correct for a girl to thank her escort at the door of her home or flat or entrance to her block of flats. It is not a social duty to ask a man in, late at night, and certainly if a girl lives alone it is not done and no man should expect it. When people get to know each other well, it is up to them and their parents what they do. But if the girl lives at home with her parents, it is courteous for her to warn them that she may bring her escort in for a hot drink before midnight, so that no one is messing about in pyjamas and no outraged father will come storming into the sitting room demanding "What is this?" Such courtesy prevents trouble at home and a great deal of embarrassment for the man of the moment.

It is now old-fashioned for anyone to expect an engagement if a couple have been going out together a number of times but, on the other hand, it is wrong for a man to take up most of a girl's time if he has no intention of marrying her. He can go on asking her out till the cows come home, but he must do so at intervals which give her the chance of meeting and going out with other people. Otherwise, broken hearts may ensue or a girl can misconstrue a friendship. It is also easier and less painful for everyone concerned to let a relationship slide if both people have a flourishing social life and are not wholly involved *all* the time.

The Breaking Up of a Friendship

One of the problems which seems to worry many women, young, not so young and even those who though "getting on", are not married and still go out alone with men friends, is how to cope with and behave on social or public occasions when a friendship is over and they have decided not to see the man again, at least not in a relationship which might involve love or marriage. They may still have to meet socially because their circles of friends coincide or they work in the same office. A great deal of embarrassment and suffering may follow unless they maintain a certain code of behaviour which at least makes them appear unconcerned in public, whatever their feelings may be.

Most women know more than one man, even if there is nothing serious between them. If this is the case, then it is wise to circulate a little in the company of an old friend who may have been let into the secret and is willing to comfort and help out. This at least shows the world that you have not retired into purdah and are still capable of enjoying life.

Here are a few rules which might help to ease embarrassing situations in connection with a problem of this nature:

1. Never say unkind or disparaging things about the man, even if you think he has treated you unjustly. This is not only extremely bad form but merely provides food for gossip and you will damage yourself more than him.

2. If you are invited out by mutual friends who may not know of the rift and ask you *both* to a party, say you would love to come but you do not know what *he* is doing. Let *them* find out. Do not give long explanations or even let a friendship with them die as they might be too embarrassed to ask you again by yourself, because you go on so much about *him*. Just act as naturally as possible, even if you feel like hell! The British are a race who are embarrassed by other people's miseries even if they honestly feel sorry for them.

3. After a rift do not see him again for a little time, even if you feel tempted to do so. You will feel so bitter that you might only try to console yourself by saying something nasty. Give yourself time to cool down and then see him again by all means—if you want to. Even throw a party and ask him and his new girl friend. Your friends will at least see that you are not going to enter a nunnery, and if he really has treated you badly he might feel a little foolish when he sees that you do not *seem* to have taken the matter too much to heart.

One benefit of a code of etiquette governing public and social behaviour in situations concerning the heart, is that it makes life much easier because, apart from personal sorrow, what makes people suffer most is hurt pride, and the old adage, "least said soonest mended" really does work.

Getting Engaged

A girl should tell her parents as soon as she has accepted a proposal, and a man should meet his future in-laws as quickly as possible (if he has not met them already), before anyone else is told. As soon as congratulations and the first gaieties of announcement are over, a man should have a talk with the girl's father about the date of their wedding, where they will live, how well off he is and his future plans and prospects. It is a matter of courtesy as well as common sense to discuss these material aspects, as it establishes mutual trust and understanding and helps to avoid all the pitfalls of a relationship involving a child who is about to leave home.

The girl's parents should always take precedence in the ensuing activities, but the man's father or mother should write to the girl's parents saying all the nice things they may wish to say. It is then up to the girl's mother to invite her daughter's future in-laws to a meal or to drinks as soon as possible. Relatives and close friends should be told before an announcement is put in the paper, otherwise they have every right to feel hurt.

The Announcement is sent to a national newspaper such as *The Times* or *The Daily Telegraph* (or a local news-paper, or both) by the girl's father and might read as follows:

Mr. James Smith and Miss Mary Jones
The engagement is announced between James Henry, younger son of Mr. and Mrs. R. D. Smith of The Lodge, Marmsworth, Hants. and Mary Caroline, only daughter of Mr. and Mrs. J. F. Jones of 5, Blank Terrace, London, S.W.3.

If the bride is a widow or divorcee, the notice should read:

> The engagement has been announced and the marriage will take place quietly between Commander R. D. Bloggs, R.N. and Mary Clegg, daughter of the late Captain G. F. Dankworth, R.N. and of Mrs. Dankworth of 34, George Crescent, Puddleton, Glos.

The Ring is a personal gift from a man to the girl he is going to marry, and need not *necessarily* be a diamond. No future bridegroom need suffer agonies from the thought that he *must* produce a diamond ring. There are many beautiful Victorian semi-precious stones which look opulent and gorgeous but cost only a few pounds.

A couple should choose the ring together. Most young people will discuss how much it would be sensible to spend on a ring but, if a man is very shy or much older than the girl, he can arrange for the jeweller to present a tray of rings all under a certain figure for her to choose, telling her that he has made a selection specially for her, but would like her to make the ultimate choice.

The Period of Engagement is usually short, three or four months, just giving time to find a home and prepare for the wedding, but this is entirely a matter of choice and circumstances.

Behaviour of the Engaged Couple. They can spend all the time in the world together but should not go away alone for a holiday or week-end, unless they do not care a hang for the feelings of their parents and the opinions of friends and acquaintances! (Going away *with* friends is a different matter). Whatever the laxity of modern life, this is still an understood rule of behaviour.

An engagement is a period when the friends of both the future bride and her groom should ask them to parties and meals, so as to meet and welcome the one they may not know. But it is not a time during which the engaged couple should indulge in selfishness or lack of manners, using the excuse that they are in love. They should not "neck" in public, hold hands all over the place or gaze into one another's eyes regardless while in other people's houses, nor should they indulge in private smiles and jokes. All the world may love a pair of attractive and charming lovers, but it will not love a couple who behave as if they were the only ones who had ever been in love, and intimate that they are slightly superior to those not in love or those who have been married some time. This could well lose them friends.

This is a time when old friendships will be consolidated and people decide whether they like the future husband or wife. So both of them should make an extra effort to be nice to their old friends and one another's friends, as these will be the basis of future friendships. Anyway, it is a particularly happy time for any engaged couple, and others, even happily married people, tend to feel slightly nostalgic and "left out" if they are treated as if they do not matter very much. It costs so little to share this happiness and to make others feel that they are part of it and of the couple's future life.

Thus all letters of congratulation should be answered immediately and as affectionately as possible, and all special parties or meals which were given to celebrate the engagement should be the subject of thank-you letters.

Breaking an Engagement is always a sad business, even

if is is for the best, and it should be dealt with as briefly as possible. Many people do not wish to make a formal announcement in the papers, saying that the marriage will not take place. There is no need to do this unless the break takes place shortly before the ceremony and there is little time to warn everyone who has been invited.

Both the man and the girl should return all wedding presents with a little note saying how grateful they are, but regret that since the marriage is not taking place they must return the present.

The girl should return her ring to the man together with any very expensive presents he has given her and he must do likewise with her presents. The old idea that a girl keeps the ring if the man breaks off the engagement is rather out of date. Unless a girl is a gold-digger and tough into the bargain, she should return the ring. If a man feels he can afford it, he may ask her to keep it.

16

WEDDINGS, BIRTHS AND FUNERALS

The Forms of Marriage

In England and Wales there are four forms of marriage: by banns, by ordinary licence, by special licence and by a registrar.

Marriage by Banns is the form most usually adopted. Banns must be called for three consecutive Sundays in the parish churches of both the future bride and the groom, unless they both live in the same parish. They must have been resident for at least fifteen days previous to the first publication of the banns. There is a small fee for the certificate of banns.

The clergyman at the church where the marriage is to take place must be notified by letter of the couple's intention to marry, of their names and addresses and how long they have resided in their parishes.

If one of the parties is a minor, a letter of consent must be obtained from both parents, and attached. (The form can be obtained from the Superintendent Registrar of the district.) If the marriage is to take place in the bride's church, a certificate of calling of the banns must be obtained from the bridegroom's parish clergyman. The marriage must then take place within three months of the banns being published.

Marriage by Ordinary Licence is a convenient alternative to the publications of banns. In London, application must be made by one party to the Faculty Office, The Sanctuary, London, S.W.1, where he will swear that he does not know of any impediment to the marriage, such as being legally married to another or consanguinous relationship, and that one of the parties has lived for at least fifteen days in the parish of the church where the marriage is to take place.

A licence is valid in England and Wales for three months after the date of issue. Outside London, it can be obtained from any Bishop's Registry Office in a cathedral town or from a Superintendent Registrar in the district of residence. The licence is granted without previous notice and is available as soon as it is issued, but the marriage must take place in a church named on the licence.

Marriage by Special Licence costs £25 and can be obtained only for special reasons such as suddenly being sent abroad. It is never granted lightly. Application must be made in person by one of the parties at the Faculty Office, Westminster, S.W.1. The marriage can then take place at any time and in any place, celebrated by the rites of the church, and residence qualifications are unnecessary.

Marriage by a Registrar can be celebrated, without any religious ceremony, at a registry office. Notice must be given by one of the parties of the intended marriage, if both have resided in the district for seven days immediately preceding the notice. If one has lived in another district, notice must be given to his or her local registrar. The certificate is issued twenty-one days after the notice has been given.

Times of Weddings. Marriages can take place in a

registered building in the presence of an authorised person between 8 a.m. and 6 p.m.

Marriages outside the Church of England, such as in a Roman Catholic church or Jewish synagogue, are not more complicated than any other marriage. The minister will know the form and so will any local registrar. The marriage can be celebrated in the place of worship, if it is within two miles of the district of the registrar issuing the licence or certificate.

Marriage in Scotland. In Scotland, people over the age of sixteen do not require their parents' consent in order to marry. Marriage is performed by a minister of any religion after the banns have been called on two Sundays in the districts where the couple have lived for at least fifteen days previously. Weddings may take place in churches or private houses, and there is no forbidden time.

Alternatively, the couple may give notice to the registrar of the district in which they have both lived for fifteen days previously. The registrar will issue a Certificate of Publication which is displayed for seven days, and it will be valid for three months in any place in Scotland.

Marriage at a registry office in Scotland requires a publication of notice for seven days or a sheriff's licence, as publication of banns is not accepted. Such a licence is immediately valid but expires after ten days. One of the parties must have lived in Scotland for at least fifteen days before the application, which is often prepared by a solicitor.

The Preparation

As soon as the wedding date has been decided the bride

will think about the kind of wedding she wants. She may wish to have a quiet one and save the money for her future home, or she may want a grand full dress affair with all the friends and relations of both families. As soon as the church has been decided upon the vicar or priest in charge should be notified and a meeting arranged with him.

The rules are not absolutely hard and fast, but generally they are as follows:

The Bride's Parents are responsible for the press announcements, the bride's dress and trousseau, flowers in the church, the reception, cars taking the bride and her father, mother and any other close members of her family to the church and photographers' fees.

The Bridegroom pays for the ring and the wedding licence, fees to the clergyman, the organist and choir, for the awning and anything else directly concerned with the service, although if there are to be orders of service, the bride's parents will have these printed at the same time as the invitations. He will pay for the bouquet for his bride and bouquets for the bridesmaids, buttonholes for his best man and ushers and any flowers worn by the bride's mother and his own mother, if they want to wear flowers—many women do not. He pays for the cars which take himself and the best man to the church and the car in which he and his bride will drive from the church to the reception. The cost of cars can, however, be divided between the parents of the bride and those of the groom, or the parents of the bride may wish to pay for it all. This is a matter for mutual arrangement.

The groom is expected to give a small present to each of the bridesmaids, and such a gift can range from a piece of jewellery to a beautifully bound book, a powder compact or any personal and pretty article.

Giving Away the Bride. The bride's father gives her away or, if he is dead or cannot be present at the ceremony, his place is taken by her brother or a close relative, or even a great family friend.

The Bridesmaids are usually the sisters, near relatives and close girl friends of the bride, and sisters of the groom. The number is purely a matter of choice but usually does not exceed six. There may be two small page-boys and four grown-up maids, or child attendants only. The bride chooses the kind of dresses her maids will wear and she may supply the material. The custom used to be for the bride's mother to pay for all the bridesmaids' dresses, but today they usually pay for their own. A girl asked to be a bridesmaid can always refuse politely if she feels she cannot afford such a dress.

There is always a chief bridesmaid who will take the bride's bouquet during the ceremony and hand it back to her before she goes into the vestry to sign the register.

The Best Man is a brother, relative or close friend of the groom, and his main duty, apart from giving moral support before the wedding, is to see to the clergyman's fees, the tips to the vergers and to hand the wedding ring to the groom in the church. He is also responsible for seeing that the bridesmaids are looked after during the reception and he should reply to any toast to the bridesmaids.

The Ushers are male relatives and friends of both bride and groom. Their duties are to stand just inside the church and ask each guest "Bride or groom?" They will place friends of the bride on the left of the aisle and friends of the groom on the right. The ushers should be at the church at least three-quarters of an hour before the ceremony, and may hand out forms of service if these are not being placed before every pew.

The Bridegroom's Clothes. When the bride is in white, the bridegroom wears morning dress with a white carnation in his buttonhole (*without* fern or silver paper).

Widows or Divorcees, when re-marrying, do not wear white, but a short dress or a pretty suit or coat. They remove their first wedding rings and never wear them again. They do not have bridesmaids or pages.

The Ceremony

The parents and close relatives of the bride and groom arrive a few minutes before the bride. The bridegroom and his best man should be in their places at least ten minutes before the service starts. The bridesmaids and pages wait in the church porch with whoever is to arrange the bride's veil before she goes up the aisle.

The bride, by tradition, arrives a couple of minutes late but this should not be exaggerated. She arrives with whoever is giving her away. The verger signals to the organist to start playing, and the bride moves up the aisle with her veil over her face (although many brides do not follow this custom). She goes in on her father's right arm, and the bridesmaids follow her according to the plan at the rehearsal the day before. The bridesmaids and ushers go to their places in the front pews during the ceremony, except for the chief bridesmaid who usually stands behind the bride and holds her bouquet.

After the ceremony the couple go into the vestry to sign the register with their parents, best man, bridesmaids and perhaps a close relation such as a grandmother. The bride throws back her veil or removes the front piece (if it is removable), the verger gives a signal to the organist and the bride and groom walk down the aisle followed by their parents and those who have signed the register. The bride's mother walks down the aisle on the left arm of the bridegroom's father and the bridegroom's mother walks down on the left arm of the bride's father (or whoever has given the bride away). Guests wait until the wedding procession has past them before leaving to go on to the reception.

The Reception

The bride's parents stand first in the receiving line, followed by the groom's parents and the bride and groom. Guests line up outside the reception room and give their names to the major-domo who will announce them. They need only shake hands and say "How do you do?" to the parents, adding perhaps a word about how lovely the bride is or how well the ceremony went. The bride introduces to her husband any friends that he may not already know, and vice versa.

The important parts of the reception are the cutting of the cake and the toast to the bride and groom. There should never be any long speeches. When all the guests have been received, the major-domo requests silence and the bride cuts the cake, with her husband's hand upon hers.

The toast to the bride and groom is usually proposed by a relative or friend of the bride. He may say, "My Lords (if any are present) ladies and gentlemen, I have pleasure in proposing the toast of the bride and bridegroom." He should not make a speech full of jokes or silly references to marriage. It should be short and dignified. The bridegroom replies with a few words of thanks. He may or may not then propose the health of the bridesmaids. The best man replies with a few words of thanks. If a meal is provided, the toasts will come at the end of it.

After the toasts the bride and groom may move around the room talking to their friends until it is time for them to go and change. When they are ready to leave, guests gather to see them off. Confetti should not be thrown, as many people object to the mess it makes, but rice and flower petals can be thrown, although often the bride and groom prefer to leave without this old custom.

The Day after the Wedding some people like to put an announcement in the papers which reads as follows:

> **Smith-Jones.** On June 4th, 1963, at the church of All Souls, Harpenden, Herts., by Canon H. Brough, David, youngest son of Major and Mrs. H. D. Smith and Mary, only daughter of Mr. and Mrs. P. Jones.

Photographers. When an announcement has appeared in the papers, local photographers will usually write and ask for permission to take photographs at the reception. The bride may like one or even two to be present at the church and later at the reception. They can move amongst the guests at the reception and take the names and addresses of all those who wish to receive copies. These are usually paid for C.O.D. or bills are sent later. No one ever pays at a reception.

Births and Christenings

When a child is born its parents may wish to announce the birth in a national or local newspaper. The announcement may read as follows:

> **Smith.** On February 12th, 1963, at St. Mary's Hospital, Paddington, to Mary, wife of James Smith, 15, Blank Terrace, S.W.3, a daughter. (The name can be added in brackets.)

The birth must be registered at the local registrar's office within six weeks in England and Wales and three weeks in Scotland. A child is usually christened in the first six months of its life. The clergyman's fee is not discussed with him as it would be for a wedding. It is a token gift sent by the father afterwards. The clergyman is always asked to any party held after the christening.

At the christening there is one godmother and two godfathers for a boy and vice versa for a girl (but no godparents are necessary at a Church of Scotland christening). The godmother always holds the baby during the ceremony and gives it to the clergyman just before he baptises it. She makes the responses during the ceremony and tells the clergyman the names when asked. The true role of godparents is to watch over the spiritual welfare of their godchildren until confirmation, or at least to show interest in them throughout their childhood.

Christening Parties. This type of party is a family affair, plus the officiating clergyman, the godparents and perhaps a few close friends. As the christening usually takes place in the early afternoon, a formal buffet tea is the best way of entertaining everyone, although some people may like to give a luncheon.

The christening cake is the *pièce de résistance* and the baby's health is drunk in champagne. The men will wear dark suits and the women smart hats and coats over an afternoon dress, or a suit.

Usually, but by no means always, the friends and relatives give a christening present. Traditionally, the godparents give a silver cup, which is probably going to be far more useful if it is a beer mug! Other presents should preferably be something intended to last a lifetime, such as a leather-bound bible or poetry book, a silver spoon or a crystal and silver scent bottle.

Funerals

Nowadays undertakers organise things to such a degree that they really do undertake to cover every detail during this very painful and difficult period, from registering the death to printing the form of service for the funeral. An obituary notice is usually sent to a national or local newspaper and inserted in the "Deaths" column. It may read as follows:

> **Smith.** On the 4th of January, 1964, at 15, Blank Road, Preston, Joan Mary Smith, beloved wife of John D. Smith and mother of Jane and Jeremy. Funeral private. (*or* Funeral service at 11 a.m. on 7th January, at St. Mary's Church, Fells Road, Preston.)

"No flowers, by request" may be added if desired.

Those who send flowers do not carry them to the house in person, but place an order with a florist to have a wreath or bunch of flowers delivered on the morning of the funeral. These should usually be sent to the church or to the undertaker, whose address can be given in the notice. A visiting card or plain card is attached, signed by the person or persons sending the flowers, together with some very simple message, "With deepest sympathy from . . ." "With all our love from . . ." or "With deepest affection from . . ."

The wearing of mourning is a purely private affair today, but certainly everyone who attends a funeral should wear black or dark grey and the men should wear black ties and hats.

Some families may wish to have a memorial service some time after a private funeral, which friends and relatives can attend. There is usually a notice in the papers indicating the time and place of the service. No cards or other notices are sent out.

It is not correct to send out printed cards to thank people for letters of condolence or flowers. These should all be acknowledged by letter, although if there are a great many a notice of thanks may be published in a newspaper, saying that all letters and flowers will be personally acknowledged in due course. For letters of condolence *see page* 19.

17

YOUR JOB

Considering that most of us work for our living and spend three-quarters of the day doing this, it seems reasonable that a code of manners should have grown up to make life at work as pleasant and smooth-running as on social occasions.

Although talent, brains and "know-how" will basically get you your job, it is an accepted fact that in jobs where relationships with other people matter the choice may fall on someone who is pleasant, sophisticated, punctilious and well-groomed rather than upon another who may have better qualifications but whose manners are boorish and who is gauche, careless and looks a mess. Knowing how to behave well also endows people with a sense of assurance, which is important when part of their job depends upon getting on with others. Courtesy really pays in *all* jobs.

(*See pages* 19-20 for letters of application for jobs.)

The Interview

This can make or break your chances, whatever your talent. Always be punctual, although there is no need to arrive twenty minutes beforehand and hang around nervously in the foyer. Let the interviewer start to talk after he has offered you a seat. Never take out a cigarette or even ask permission to smoke unless a cigarette is offered you. Smile when you go in and shake hands. Make yourself *feel* there is a pleasant expectant look upon your face and do not give the impression that the whole thing is too boring for words. Many people give this impression because they are nervous and do not want to appear so. A smile on any face at least shows interest and the desire to please. (Otherwise, why should you be going to the interview anyway?)

Do not talk loudly or whisper so that everything you say has to be repeated. Do not go on and on, or answer in monosyllables. Just talk normally and sell yourself and your talents without overdoing it.

If you are a woman, never flirt or make the interviewer feel that you are flaunting your attractions. This is death to a job, unless the interviewer is the sort of man you would probably not want to work for later on!

If you are a man, do not talk about your wife or private life unless you are asked to do so. Do not make the mistake of thinking that to appear "business-like" you must be cold, formal and almost unfriendly. Many people give an utterly false impression of themselves because they are afraid to appear natural and friendly. There is a great deal of difference between familiarity and a normal and pleasant approach. On the other hand, it is almost worse to be familiar and "take over" the interview. The interviewer is the one who handles the situation. He is offering a position and a salary and you are offering yourself. The risk is more on his side than on yours.

There is no reason under the sun why you should not ask any question you wish, after you have been questioned and answered satisfactorily. You can ask about the firm, your possible position in it, your salary and prospects, any travelling which may be involved, the amount of holiday and the hours of work. But ask these questions more or less in that order. It looks very odd if a person being interviewed immediately starts asking

143

questions about money, holidays and hours of work before finding out what he can do for the firm for which he is to *work*.

A letter of thanks for an interview should be handwritten.

On the Job

In all positions of trust, or if you hold any senior job, you are almost on your honour not to cheat about the hours you keep, the number of personal telephone calls you make and the time you waste. No one can cheat for ever without detection, although he may get away with it for some time. Besides, it is unfair to the firm and a sign that you are really not very interested in the job.

Even if you feel no one notices how punctilious you are, there is always the personal satisfaction that you are doing the job properly, and such punctiliousness makes you into the kind of person who shows it, even if you are not aware of this. It will also show in your work in the long run.

Office Relationships

You should not start calling others by their Christian names unless you are specifically asked to do so. If you are in a fairly senior position where you might call your boss by his Christian name, it is courteous when addressing him or talking about him in front of juniors to call him "Mr." There is always a definite hierarchy in any institution, office or factory and to observe it with courtesy and simplicity, but without fawning or crawling, will avoid ill-feeling. It is also very short-sighted to play politics in an office, to take sides or talk disparagingly of others. Discretion, tact and a sense of diplomacy have done more to further people in their jobs than occasional flashes of brilliance.

Unhappy in Your Job

Unless you are determined to leave for a specific reason or your unhappiness is the result of something you feel cannot be put right, you should give your boss the benefit of the doubt and ask to see him to discuss your position. Any boss worth his salt wants to know the reason why members of the staff are not satisfied. This may mean your going straight to the boss, to your immediate superior in the office or to a personnel officer.

This attitude of interest in the staff is part of what is called "management," and it is the duty of any boss to see that all goes smoothly in an office and that employees are used to the best of their capacities. But never circumvent your immediate superior to complain to someone above him or her. This will not make a good impression on anyone. It will make an enemy of those who work just above you and dub you as untrustworthy and a tale-bearer to those at the top.

Asking for a Rise

If you have a good reason to ask for a rise, it is foolish to sit and feel discontented because you are afraid to ask. Money is the main incentive to work, and every boss knows this. Salaries are an important aspect of any job.

It is wise to marshal all your reasons and any facts relevant to a rise, and to put them forward politely and reasonably. The answer can be "Yes" or "No", but no one need fear getting the sack merely because he asks for more money, although bosses are not *always* perfect. (You must remember this before you rush into an interview which may put you in an awkward spot.)

Do not give an ultimatum by intimating that either you get a rise or you will leave. This puts your boss into an equally difficult position, especially if you do not really *mean* to leave.

The Secretary

The secretary's job is one where the daily employee/boss relationship can be the most difficult. It can also be the most pleasant. A secretary should always be discreet and courteous. She can be friendly but never familiar. If she is familiar in front of others, it puts her boss in a bad light and this is often the start of her downfall.

She should not be afraid of her boss, so that she fears asking him to repeat an instruction or some dictation. She is not expected to be a thought-reader or to be perfect. She should not be afraid of saying she has made a mistake. Most people, unless they are tyrants or unreasonable, would much rather a secretary told them of any mistakes which could be remedied, than that the results of a mistake piled up until the consequences became really serious.

A secretary should be very discreet with the rest of the office about her boss's work, his movements and the people he sees. She should see that his correspondence and personal papers are always covered up, so that those who enter the office are not tempted to look at them. Neither should she be the office gossip, repeating to her boss everything that goes on. This would soon become known and not only endanger her position but the relationship of her boss with the rest of the staff.

A secretary should be particularly courteous on the telephone, as she is not representing herself alone but her boss and her firm.

A good secretary is a screen protecting her boss from unnecessary interruptions and discussions. She should soothe irate callers, and in other cases, try to deal with routine matters herself.

A secretary should under no circumstances fall into a relationship with her boss which might cause gossip.

Apart from appearing pleasant and efficient, a secretary should make a special effort to memorise the names of those who call or are colleagues and acquaintances of her boss. This makes them feel important and is one of the best secrets of good public relations she can learn.

A boss should treat his secretary in a friendly but not a familiar way. He should not use her as an errand girl to do his personal chores or those of his wife, unless he is really "pushed" and asks her assistance as a personal favour.

Manners in the Office

Manners at work should basically be the same as good manners at home or at school. You should always look pleasant and greet those you pass in the corridors with a smile, even if you do not know them well enough to talk. (Many a person has been noticed in a large organisation because she always looked pleasant and greeted others courteously.)

It is also an attractive trait if you are prepared to help or suggest someone who can help with a problem presented by a colleague. "That's not my job" will never further good relationships or help you move up the ladder. If you belong to a firm it is your job to help in any way you can. This also earns you the reputation of being someone who can be depended upon in an emergency or when things are difficult. It is really an attitude of mind, rather than constantly doing work which is not your own. Never put up a barrier of resentment before you know exactly what is involved.

Changing Your Job

In a free country everyone has the right to move on to another job or occupation whenever they wish. But some consideration and courtesy is necessary. Do not march into your boss's room and say "I'm leaving next week." Ask for a personal interview and say you wish to leave. Do him the courtesy of explaining why. After all, he has employed you for a time and has the right to know why you wish to move elsewhere. It also gives him the chance of righting any wrong which may have motivated your move, or of deciding that you are such a good person that he might well want to have you back some day.

Even if there is a specified time of notice, it is courteous to ask if this is convenient and to offer to stay (if at all possible) until such time as it is. If, on the other hand, you have a job where it is imperative that you start on a certain date, explain the reason fully, apologise for any inconvenience and ask if you can help in any way, such as staying on to work late or searching for a replacement.

The important thing is to leave pleasantly and to leave a good impression, having caused the least possible inconvenience. Apart from being a basic courtesy in business life, it is one which can easily pay future dividends.

Should you need a reference for the future, you ask your present boss if he would be willing to give you one in writing or on the telephone at some future date. Do not take it for granted that he will praise you to the skies without being warned. However good you may have been, if you treat him in a cavalier fashion you intimate that you have ceased to respect him, merely because you do not happen to work for him any more. This will not endear you to anyone.

If you have been given the sack, you have every right to

know the reason why and to ask for an interview with your boss or whoever hired you in the first place. You have the right to justify yourself, to give any explanations you feel might mitigate your situation and to ask to be given proper notice so that you can find another job. No boss has the right to refuse you a reference, but in some circumstances you may feel it wise not to insist.

If you are giving someone else the sack, you should remember his dignity as a human being, however much you feel you want to get rid of him. For the moment that person is absolutely in your power, so you must be specially careful to be honest, courteous and as kind as possible according to the circumstances. If you tell the complete truth few people resent it, and many are grateful. Sacking, like getting out of a love affair, is not a situation where men are at their best. The tendency is to slide as quickly as possible from an unpleasant situation or to "pass the buck." Every human being has the *right* to know why he or she is being discarded and has the right to a personal interview with a superior.

18

GOING ON HOLIDAY

If you are not making arrangements entirely through a travel agency, you should write to the hotel of your choice a fair time before you intend to go on holiday. If the hotel is abroad, it is better to write in English than in pidgin anything else! Most people engaged in the hotel business can get letters translated easily. If you can type the letter, all the better, as it will be clearer. List your questions in paragraphs so that they are easy to answer. If the reply is to your satisfaction, confirm your reservation as quickly as possible.

It is also wise to write a postcard a week before you arrive, reiterating the day and time of your arrival, and stating whether you will require a meal if you are to arrive at a time when meals may not be served. This is courteous and will make doubly sure that you get a warm welcome. Any cancellation of arrangements should be made as quickly as possible.

Should the hotel be a large one, you might ask whether they dress in the evenings (especially at winter sports resorts). This does not mean you *have* to do so, but will save you the embarrassment of arriving with quite unsuitable clothes.

Always take a scarf, cardigan or jacket to cover your head and arms if you are going to a Latin country where you might be visiting churches, as bare arms and head can cause offence.

Women should not wear slacks, jeans or shorts when

entering churches or walking around large towns (other than seaside resorts) unless it appears to be customary. The more the place is a tourist centre, the more sophisticated are the local people, although bikinis are not always welcome in Spain and certain parts of Italy.

It is wise to take a small phrase book even if you fancy yourself as a linguist. For a simple request a colloquial phrase is always understood better than a somewhat archaic translation out of the schoolroom. Never get annoyed if people cannot understand you, and don't shout because you think they will understand better (this is a common fallacy). Do not discuss others in their presence because you think they will not understand you. Such is the sensitivity of human nature that an Eskimo will sense an unpleasant remark made in Swahili.

Work out your tips carefully with the leaflet issued by your bank listing small sum exchanges. You can always ask a good travel agent the form about tipping in certain countries. For instance, in France, Italy, Spain and Belgium usherettes are tipped in both cinemas and theatres. Most other tipping is done on the 10% to 15% basis, but look at your bills to see whether service is included. If it is, you do not *have* to tip in restaurants or hotels.

In Latin countries you may find that servants, drivers and touts always appear to be asking or waiting around for tips, but sometimes they depend upon them for a living more than their opposite numbers at home. Give smaller tips but more often. It is much better to inquire about tipping in various countries, either from your travel agent or from a hall porter, than to find yourself shouted at.

In most countries there is a fixed tariff for railway porters.

In France you always tip a wine waiter as well as your table waiter (unless a service charge appears on the bill).

(For further notes on tipping *see pages* 108-110.)

Manners Abroad

Each year more and more of us are travelling abroad, either on business or on pleasure. "When in Rome do as the Romans do" can be a dangerous maxim to follow, as it can lead to some rather odd behaviour on the part of people who do not *really* know the customs of another country.

The important thing is to be as courteous and thoughtful as possible and to keep your eyes open to see how others behave. It does not go down well to be more Italian than the Italians or more American than the Americans. Basic courtesies are the same in all civilised countries, although customs may differ. It looks foolish to follow them to a T, such as cutting up your food and eating it with a fork as in America or kissing ladies' hands as in France. It will only make others think you are a "phoney."

Act as you would in your own country. On the other hand, the bumptious and overbearing person who treats all foreigners as if they were idiots, or shouts because he thinks they will understand better, is a nauseating product and does no good at all as an ambassador of his country. There is a happy medium between paying respect to the customs of the country and overdoing it. Keep a sense of proportion.

Psychologically, a business trip abroad is an escape from the routine of life at home, but it is not an excuse for living it up. Businessmen from all countries make this mistake, and it does not make a particularly good impression on the people of the country they are visiting.

Flirting with secretaries and other people's wives is a

great social sin, and in some countries it may be construed as a deadly insult and ruin a business deal.

It is also unattractive to brag too much about one's own country. However much you long to boost it, this will only madden foreigners. Keep a sense of proportion. On the other hand, do not run down your country under the impression that you are making yourself sympathetic to foreigners, and thereby paying a compliment to their country by intimating that it is superior. This is foolish and may well be interpreted literally.

An intelligent interest in their country and an intelligent explanation of yours create a far better impression than unadulterated sales talk.

British businessmen who are going abroad on export affairs can obtain from the Board of Trade excellent pamphlets on individual countries called "Hints to Businessmen Visiting. . . ." These can be purchased for 2s. each from the Board of Trade (Commercial Relations and Exports Department), Horse Guards Avenue, London, S.W.1. They give information about climate, clothing, currency, etiquette, passports, visas, travel, hotels, restaurants, interpreter and translation services, tipping, trade and industry and a great many more infinitely useful details.

If you have been given an introduction to someone abroad, do write and warn him that you will be arriving on a certain date and staying at a particular place. Too many people from all countries arrive and telephone out of the blue, with a "Yoo-hoo, I'm here, entertain me." However much others may wish to be courteous, you must remember that they have private lives and commitments and cannot drop everything for you. Indeed, this approach is quite likely to make them very angry.

There are a few small points which it is wise to assess before going abroad on a business trip. They may seem unimportant to you but matter to the peoples concerned. For instance in Belgium and Holland it is customary to send hostesses flowers after a meal in a private house. The Finns are demons for punctuality and to arrive three minutes late is almost an insult. In France you shake hands with everyone you meet and always start a conversation with "Bonjour Madame" or "Bonjour Monsieur." It is well worth while doing some research among friends and acquaintances at home before you set out on your trip.

Index